The Greek word for "repent" can be more richly translated as "to reshape the heart; to think differently." Sam Brown models how to do both, in tender, compelling stories that are deeply personal and profoundly universal. His at times searing vulnerability is our gain in this edifying and moving memoir.

—Terryl Givens, coauthor of
The Christ Who Heals and *The God Who Weeps*

God is real. Christ is real. Love is real. We belong to one another. Sam Brown not only recounts his spiritual journey to arrive at these simple but inexhaustible truths but invites the reader to join with him in opening up to the possibilities inherent in a God-drenched world. These probing and moving essays show what can happen when a brilliant mind meets the refinement of a beautiful soul. The Latter-day Saint community is richer, and the world is truer, because Sam Brown has chosen the life of faith.

—Patrick Mason, author of *Planted: Belief and Belonging in an Age of Doubt* and *Restoration: God's Call to the 21st-Century World*

Where the Soul Hungers

A
Living Faith
Book

LIVING FAITH books are for readers who cherish the life of the mind and the things of the Spirit. Each title is a unique example of faith in search of understanding, the voice of a scholar who has cultivated a believing heart.

OTHER LIVING FAITH BOOKS INCLUDE:

Adam S. Miller, *Letters to a Young Mormon* (2nd ed.)

Samuel M. Brown, *First Principles and Ordinances: The Fourth Article of Faith in Light of the Temple*

Steven L. Peck, *Evolving Faith: Wanderings of a Mormon Biologist*

Patrick Q. Mason, *Planted: Belief and Belonging in an Age of Doubt*

Ashley Mae Hoiland, *One Hundred Birds Taught Me to Fly: The Art of Seeking God*

George B. Handley, *If Truth Were a Child*

Thomas F. Rogers, *Let Your Hearts and Minds Expand: Reflections on Faith, Reason, Charity, and Beauty*

Melissa Wei-Tsing Inouye, *Crossings: A Bald Asian American Latter-day Saint Woman Scholar's Ventures through Life, Death, Cancer & Motherhood (Not Necessarily in That Order)*

George B. Handley, *The Hope of Nature: Our Care for God's Creations*

Where the Soul Hungers

*one doctor's journey
from atheism to faith*

SAMUEL MORRIS BROWN

BYU Maxwell Institute   DESERET BOOK

The paper used in this publication meets the minimum requirements of the American National Standard for Information Sciences—Permanence of Paper for Printed Library Materials. ANSI Z39.48-19

ISBN: 978-1-9503-0404-2

Art direction: Blair Hodges

Cover design: Heather Ward

Book design: Carmen Durland Cole

Printed in the United States of America

http://maxwellinstitute.byu.edu

Library of Congress Cataloging-in-Publication Data
Names: Brown, Samuel Morris, author.
Title: Where the soul hungers : one doctor's journey from atheism to faith / Samuel Morris Brown.
Description: Provo, UT : Neal A. Maxwell Institute for Religious Scholarship, [2021] | Includes index. | Summary: "Though raised as a Latter-day Saint in Utah, Samuel Morris Brown was an atheist from an early age, and proud of it. Yet, by his own account, God became an undeniable presence in his life. His conversion to the faith of his forebears happened by degrees, and today he is joyfully living a life in Christ. In this volume, Sam Brown narrates a number of the waypoints on his journey into believing and belonging. Some of those moments are dramatic, but many are composed of small and simple things, which take on profound significance as Sam reflects on them now in these pages. With gentle, self-critical humor and a generous regard for those who have accompanied him on his way, this book by Sam Brown is an offer to walk with you a while on your own journey of faith"—Provided by publisher.
Identifiers: LCCN 2020036957 | ISBN 9781950304042 (paperback)
Subjects: LCSH: Brown, Samuel Morris. | Mormons—Biography. | LCGFT: Autobiographies.
Classification: LCC BX8695.B73 B76 2021 | DDC 289.3092 [B]—dc23
LC record available at https://lccn.loc.gov/2020036957

Contents

Contents

Introduction

I'm still haunted by a woman who died in our intensive care unit years ago. She was eighteen weeks pregnant and had a kidney infection serious enough that her lungs failed. She quickly ended up on maximal life support, barely hanging on. We diagnosed the Acute Respiratory Distress Syndrome (ARDS). That's by far the most common and expected scenario for someone whose lungs stop working during a serious infection, and pregnant women's lungs are notoriously prone to this problem. We treated her with everything we could, but she showed no glimmer of improvement. Her body had stumped all our best thinking and treatments. In desperation, we decided to pretend that we didn't know what we thought we knew. What if, we forced ourselves to wonder, we were asking the wrong questions all along?

Allowing ourselves new eyes, we realized that a subtle shadow on a heart ultrasound was not what it had seemed to be on our first review. Her underlying problem was an infected heart valve. As cruel fate had it in this case, the heart valve couldn't be fixed; she died three days later. Even though our mistake didn't determine her terrible outcome, I've never forgotten the moment I realized that we'd been asking the wrong questions. We had fallen prey to what cognitive psychologists call "framing errors" and "anchoring bias," among other scientific-sounding terms. We'd focused on the kidney infection and missed the subtler but far more important problem of the heart valve. That lesson has stayed with me, both in medicine and in my scholarly work on religious history. I've come to realize that many of the problems we struggle with are due to selective blindness.

One area where I sense a substantial and growing blindness is in how we in this current age—with its glistening technology and accompanying ecological crisis, of individual self-fashioning and ruptured communities, of public secularism and private spiritual distress—tend to think about God and life in God. Entire categories of belief and life have been classified as outside the scope of polite society. Some philosophers talk about the current state of culture as "modern" or "late modern."

The word "modern" can mean many different things. Some of us will remember modernism as referring to art or literature in early twentieth-century England or America. Others will think of eighteenth-century French politics or the controversies over theology and the Bible that led to Protestant fundamentalism in the early twentieth century. For many, "modern" is a neutral word that just means that something is sophisticated or new.

I tend to use "modern" in a fairly specific way. I borrow the underlying concepts from the Christian philosopher Charles Taylor, who describes the dominant view of the world in Europe and America over the last fifty years as "secular."[1] I find that "secular" has become so charged with conflicting, secondary meanings that it's hard to use it outside scholarly settings. At its core, secular just means this-worldly concerns,

---

1. Charles Taylor, *A Secular Age* (Cambridge, MA: Harvard University Press, 2007).

that which is bound in time. The secular is what relates to human (rather than divine) beings. As long as it exists in harmony with the divine realm, the secular is necessary and beautiful. But in certain increasingly visible parts of Western culture after the Protestant Reformation and the European Enlightenment, an ideology gained momentum, a system of belief that tried to substitute the secular alone for the unity of secular and sacred. This use of secular has become a catchphrase and battle slogan, and I find "modern" a bit less fraught.

We religious folk have been shaped by these modern views as much as—if in somewhat different ways than—our peers who see themselves as nonreligious. Even where people continue to believe in God, they do so in different language, with new constraints on the kinds of thoughts they can think and lives they can live. I consider many modern ideas in these essays, often with an eye to blind spots. Without burrowing into an academic rabbit hole, I see three potential dark sides of modern ideologies.

First, modern ideology advances the belief that the temporal can be completely separated from the spiritual. While this resurrects an old pagan philosophy, its dominance is largely a product of the last couple centuries of European history. One classic example of the basic impulse was the Deist belief that God existed but was hopelessly remote from human experience. With God safely banished to a remote corner of the universe, it became easier to maintain that the earthly, material aspects of existence could stand entirely on their own. What had previously been one-half of a harmony of interwoven realms was meant to stand alone. This was no clean surgery to remove an unwanted growth from a body, as many of its partisans believed, but a cutting of a person down the middle. It is a fiction to imagine that we need nothing other than mere physical matter to live in and make sense of the world, but this fiction seems to gain traction day by day in Western culture.

Second, we have the idea that selves must be insulated from communities through an "authentic" individualism. We in the West are prone to talk now about personal authenticity and to assume the worst about institutions. Many moderns worry that individuals will drown in community and that we are the only ones who can possibly know ourselves. Traditionally religious folk have sometimes also heard the call of extreme individualism. The consequences of this acute independence can be profound. We moderns experience profound alienation and loneliness: England now has a Ministry of Loneliness, and companies now rent fake family members to clients in need. Even self-identified secularists—despite their philosophical roots in modern individualism—have begun to fret about the depth of the separation of people from each other.

A third estrangement attempts to separate reason from God and humanity, to "detach" thinking from its contexts in human life and spiritual aspiration. Reason, increasingly considered synonymous with "science" (a nebulous concept on the best day), is held to be the basis of all experience, strength, and meaning. This aspect of modernism affects many of us within the churches too, shaping the approaches we may take to doctrine or defenses of our belief. This rationalist approach has been helpful in many respects, especially when it comes to certain technologies. But it is only one mode of reasoning, which is itself a subset of human behavior and experience. This particular form of brain activity does not have the depth and capacity to serve in the place of God.

I've highlighted three important problems with modern thought; there are others I haven't mentioned. But wonderful things have also come in the last century or so. And we will have to admit that even though believers have been at the forefront of many campaigns—like abolition or women's suffrage—good cultural changes also came from people who disliked Christian churches. As crazy and dangerous as our world feels sometimes, it is on average much less cruel than it used to be. The aversion to cruelty and the love of marginalized people is in many respects the legacy of Jesus Christ. It was Jesus who loved above all others the poor, the forgotten, the people who are at the bottom of traditional power relationships. We should welcome any voice that gives us additional insight or strength in the quest to follow Jesus in restoring the world. Sometimes the critics of Christianity have seen to the heart of our world better than we churchgoers have. There's more than enough blindness to go around.

So where does this leave us? The modern age has brought much terror, blindness, and stupidity. But it has also brought less tolerance for cruelty and, in important ways, has pointed out where we believers have ourselves been blind. Many of us will thus find ourselves cross-pressured between two worlds.

My story may be useful as a way of considering possible ways forward. I freely admit that I'm no great person. But my soul is hungry for the presence of God, and my path through life may be familiar to others who are similarly torn. In a story I've told before and will continue to tell, I'm a lapsed atheist. Liberation from atheism was the first great opening of the world to my view. That initial experience of learning to see made possible the greater love and vision that came many years later in the aftermath of my wife's cancer diagnosis. Therein lies another important story.

Several of these essays have grown in the soil of my recently broken heart. Even those that fail to mention the family health crisis that jolted me from the numbly busy life of a physician scientist have been shaped by that calamity. Love and vulnerability are touchstones of human beauty, and they can come into rare clarity when life is threatened. Such was the case with me. As I mention this fact, I want to be careful. I don't want to trade in the suffering of my beloved wife. We all too often are prone to see the suffering of others as something to profit by, whether it's the satisfaction of our curiosity or the status that is sometimes accorded the sufferer. I love my wife with my whole soul; the painful betrayal of her body by the cancerous cells of her eye is her story to tell, not mine.

Still, the reality stands: light and grace have gained easier access to my broken heart than to my comfortably proud one. My heart and mind have been remade in tragedy. My willingness to doubt common cultural assumptions probably comes in part because I realized how little late modern culture has to contribute to understanding the hard problems of existence. I know because I had to solve those problems, my eyes open to the full range of possible solutions. The modern culture we've inherited visibly failed at the task. The essays collected here arise from the fact that tragedy has made me willing to tear off my blinders. The illusions by which we now so often live have shown me their true colors.

I'm also a reader-writer who knows what it's like to live in the intense cross-pressures between worlds and cultures. In all this hunger and tension, I abide in Christ with my whole heart. I stand in temple covenant, in the Latter-day Saint remnant of the Garden at Eden, eager for God and the love of the Saints. These essays represent an attempt to bring secular and sacred back together, to end the separation and let divine and human reason live together in me.

These essays cover a range of topics. Their variety is meant to show some of the range of thinking, feeling, and loving made possible within the restored gospel. Our Restoration forebears were right when they claimed that the gospel is vast and can accommodate the entire spectrum of truth. Within their diversity, these essays share fundamental concerns. In them I try to consider what it means to be a person of faith in our late modern world. I try to offer alternatives to the modern party lines, to resist the great separations of spiritual from temporal, of people from communities, and of reason from life.

The temporal and the spiritual belong together. They always have, and they always will. As I discuss further in the first essay, "Life Is a Funny Place," I want to lead and share a life that scintillates between heaven and earth. "Scintillates" can sound like I'm talking about wearing makeup with glitter. That's not what I mean, although I'm father to creative children, and I don't mind a little glitter. When I talk about scintillation, I mean bouncing back and forth between the human and divine realms. I want to allow heaven and earth to weave together without requiring that they be used up in the process.

This observation isn't new with me. The Anglican priest and Bible scholar N. T. Wright argues that the interweaving of heaven and earth is the core message of the New Testament.[2] In a less scriptural vein, my daughter's favorite poet, T. S. Eliot, evoked something similar in his *Four Quartets*. In his own tortured and melancholy way, I hear him yearning for scintillation when he talks about being

> At the still point of the turning world. Neither flesh nor
> fleshless;
> Neither from nor towards; at the still point, there the
> dance is.[3]

That dance that is neither flesh nor fleshless is what I'm trying to live and share. I'm trying to ask the question "What does it feel like, in full view of contemporary culture, to know that this world exists in harmony with another?"

I also find in the restored gospel the promise that we can be made whole as individuals within the self-giving love of sacred relation. As I explore at length in the essay "In Praise of the Inauthentic Life," many of us have been on a fool's errand, seeking ourselves where only half a person could ever be. We are truly and fully embodied, truly and fully ourselves, within

---

2.   N. T. Wright, *How God Became King: The Forgotten Story of the Gospels* (San Francisco: HarperOne, 2012).

3.   T. S. Eliot, *Four Quartets*, quartet 1, "Burnt Norton."

the body of Christ. In "What of the Wisdom of Solomon?" I consider what obligations others impose upon us with their grief. The gospel will not leave us alone.

I also explore ways of thinking with God. I wouldn't be offended if some readers thought of these essays as "apologetic," because they are. Apologetics are concerned with providing supportive contexts for belief. They aren't "apologies" in the sense of being sorry for doing something wrong, but attempts to represent as honestly as we can why it is that we live and believe in a particular way. In my view, some traditional Latter-day Saint apologetic strategies have relied heavily on modern rationalism. Assuming that current approaches to rationality and its foundational role are correct, in other words, they have worked out potential solutions for believers. They've done so for ultimately religious reasons, and they have generally done so in good faith, whatever their critics might say. Their strategy makes some sense—detached rationalism is a common feature of our culture, so it has made sense to use that language. Such approaches almost certainly worked in the middle twentieth century and continue to work for some believers even now. When I was trying to find my footing as a new Latter-day Saint believer in the 1990s, for example, I found Hugh Nibley a godsend. There is much to love in those traditions. But for many now, this placement of God secondary to reason can make it difficult for us to think God in the modern world.

Here I'm inverting the usual direction of apologetics. Instead of asking how to think about God from within modern rationalism, I'm wondering how we might make sense of *our thinking* within a world charged by the presence of God. I'm proposing that we have been prone to look at the wrong things, like our medical team treating the pregnant woman with an infected heart valve. The questions I want to pose are these: What might it be like to think from within the experience of

God's encompassing vastness? What might the possibility of divine communion have on our perception of the world? Asking and trying to answer these questions may offend some entrenched ideas about reason and religion. But I've come to believe that these ideas call for our earnest and godly skepticism.

With those caveats in mind, I've realized that part of what is holding back some of my friends, family, and neighbors when it comes to religious belief and identity is the lack of descriptions of religious lives that could make sense to them. Too many of our peers have been taught to think that greedy televangelists and spittle-soaked antigay protestors are the only people who remain in the churches. These partisan stories about religion are wrong—the range of soulful and life-giving religious belief and practice is vast, diverse, and breathtakingly lovely. All types of people in all sorts of shapes are religious, including kind conservative intellectuals as well as head-in-the-clouds liberal professors, libertarian factory workers, and starry-eyed political activists. We as a Latter-day Saint community haven't always imagined that we have examples readily at hand of religious people who are also intellectuals, but I am both. I make my living by my wits as a medical professor, and I'm steadfastly religious.

These essays are prayerful reflections on President Dieter F. Uchtdorf's 2013 call to "doubt your doubts."[4] While he didn't provide many details in this wise and beautiful sermon, I think that the doubts President Uchtdorf calls us to doubt are our thoughtless acceptance of the cultural assumptions that have driven our culture in recent decades, often under the banner of "reason" or "science." I'm suggesting that there are some pretty important reasons to doubt the *posture* of doubt; I offer several of these reasons to doubt doubt in these essays. I'm not remotely suggesting that having doubts or struggles

---

4.   Dieter F. Uchtdorf, "Come, Join with Us," *Ensign*, May 2013, 23.

or anxious wonderings is a moral failing. For heaven's sake, I've experienced all of that and more. I've been an atheist, an agnostic, and a conflicted believer for many decades. However fervent and sincere, my faith has never been natural or spontaneous for any sustained period. Belief without doubt has never come naturally to me, and I suspect it never will. God does not ask that we sacrifice our ability to wonder and probe and question. God asks for our sincere love and our willingness to spread that renewing love to the world. Doubt is morally neutral, neither good nor bad. But the contemporary ideology of doubt seems to be confusing us about the nature of doubt in our own lives and communities. Having doubts and struggles of faith is par for the course for many of us. Genuine love often requires some acknowledgement of those doubts. But to make of doubt a religion in its own right is to put fashionable blinders on. The cultures of doubt can blind us to much truth and goodness.

By coming at contemporary culture from a different perspective less wedded to modern-style rationalism, I don't mean to give the impression that I position myself beyond belief. On the contrary. I believe the way I breathe. I believe with my whole hungry soul. I haven't always believed, and I don't believe everything. I'm natively a skeptic. But my skepticism is strong enough to doubt the ideologies that often pass for a cultural status quo. More importantly, I've let myself be open to possibility and meaning based in the sacred reality of relationships. In that willingness to be open about the possibility of religious faith and experience, I find myself believing more than I ever thought I would.

These essays have diverse life histories. Some began life on Latter-day Saint websites, magazines, or blogs; others started life as firesides at university institutes. They have been extensively revised here. Many are newly written for this collection. Some of these essays are pure devotions—attempts to describe what a life of heaven-and-earth worship feels like. Others are more philosophical, poking at the conceptual tangles that are turning into ever-more-elaborate Gordian knots in Western culture. I hope that these more philosophical essays also confirm or expand possibilities for living religiously. Other essays are attempts to repent, admissions of times and ways that I have fallen short. Still others celebrate life and the senses. I've divided them into sections to make it easier to settle into a few related meditations on a quiet Sunday afternoon. I hope that together these stories and essays give a sense for what one academic Latter-day Saint life looks like when the divine realm is allowed access to this world of toil and wonder. This scintillation in the company of the Saints is the great treasure of my life. This life in the Restoration is the truest thing I know.

PART ONE:
LIFE'S STORIES

Life Is a Funny Place

One of my clearest memories from childhood is of my father forcing me to be baptized as a Latter-day Saint at age eight. I glared as he cajoled me into the font. My powerless and wordless rage finally expressed itself in tears, which he interpreted as the testimony of the Holy Spirit. I remember nothing about the baptism itself, just the conviction that I would thenceforth live a double life: strenuous atheist on the inside and practitioner compliant with Latter-day Saint rites of passage on the outside—like a chocolate bonbon filled with horseradish.

As my father moved from the orbit of our family, a journey completed when my mother divorced him when I was twelve, my atheism became more obvious and insistent. I was quick-witted and read widely, including stacks of anti-Mormon pamphlets. I believed that I could dance verbal circles around any of the people in my neighborhood. I considered myself a French existentialist. I loved how insolent my existentialism was, how casually it shrugged its shoulders at religious folk. I didn't understand much of the actual philosophy, but I cherished it anyway. The scandal of my atheism filled me with pride.

That adolescent system of belief and practice collapsed when I was eighteen.

When I wrote a book about the fourth article of faith for the Neal A. Maxwell Institute's Living Faith Series, the editor told me that I needed to begin with a compelling story about my personal faith. I decided to tell the story of my first clear encounter with God, after which I could no longer imagine myself as an atheist or agnostic. My friends and family had prayed for me for years, and in response to their prayers my heart mellowed. I discovered the God against whom I had been closing my eyes all those years. It's a familiar enough story: *God scares the hell out of an atheist.* It was basically the Alma the Younger conversion story set in a small town in Davis County, Utah, in 1990. I didn't fall into a trance like Alma did, but I may as well have. The Spirit jolted me out of my former life. Nothing of any importance could remain as it had been. God *was*, and I'd come to know that. As it turned out, my editor liked the story, and so did readers. For some, it's been their favorite part of the book.[1]

That conversion story was true as far as it went; it all happened as I reported it. But the full story of my faith is much more gnarled than I could communicate in an attention-grabbing opener for a popular theology book. Nothing is ever that simple. Where that conversion sounds effortless, with God changing my life from the outside, the reality is that faith involves a great deal of work. Faith always does.

I've grown tired in adulthood of arguments about faith versus works. I know that many Protestants have felt like this opposition is more important than almost anything else. But the opposition doesn't make sense to me. Faith is work, and a

1. Samuel Morris Brown, *First Principles and Ordinances: The Fourth Article of Faith in Light of the Temple* (Provo, UT: Neal A. Maxwell Institute for Religious Scholarship, 2014).

lot of it. That's the nature of faith. And work makes faith real in the world. The two are as inextricable as body is from spirit or grace is from love. Neither lives apart from the other; both express, develop, and admire the love of God.

I've spent three decades now choosing the life of faith. Sometimes I do it well; sometimes I do it poorly. And, crucially, I've done that work with my mind and my heart. As a believer who is also a scholar, I draw on reason and the spirit as I work my faith. As I reflect on my story as a disciple-scholar (to borrow a term from the late apostle Elder Neal A. Maxwell), I've realized that several principles guide my work of faith.

1. What's missing is often what's most important.

I spent my decade of atheism viewing myself as a clear-sighted intellectual. This attitude wasn't original with me; I'd borrowed the fear underlying that posture from the world around me. This attitude expresses itself as engaging the world unfettered by the traditions or the experiences of others. We want to see past old superstitions; we don't want to be duped. Clear sight is generally a treasure. But this aspiration has created a blind spot that can extend all the way to eternity. At some point, some of us began to believe that if we can't see something easily and clearly, then it doesn't exist. We lost the ability to see what's missing. This blindness is bad for both religion and science. It's as if we are sailors in the merchant marine who believe that nothing exists beneath the surface of the sea. We risk believing that the tip is the entire iceberg, when the truth is that *what's missing is often what's most important.*

When I abandoned atheism, I realized that I could choose to see God in and through the world. And once I allowed that possibility, it was as if the life under the ocean's surface flashed into view—the fish and whales and plants and mountains and trenches. I'd discovered a new realm. What had once been the shadowy and indistinct undulations of the sea proved to be an overwhelming glory. I saw people in a different light—not as talking animals who wear shoes, but as shimmering goddesses and gods in embryo. I had learned to see what others refused to.

This capacity to see is precisely the gift that the prophets and prophetesses bring to us from the presence of God. They can see things that aren't there. It might be the remote past or the distant future. It might be a moral aspect of our current life that is invisible to the broader society. It might be the revelation of the majesty of God that evades routine vision but courses through the entire world. It's one of the great delusions of our age, this idea that everything is precisely as it seems, that the world is skin deep. Faith, under the tutoring of scripture, prayer, and church service, opens up that actual world to our view.

2. The framing is often more important than the question.

I arrived at Harvard College about a month after I became a believer. It was a marvelous time for me in a million different ways. I'd never had such easy access to learning and learned people. I discovered the terrors of homelessness through friends who joined our singles ward Sunday dinner. I began to work within the community, covering the Sunday night shift in a homeless shelter (donating my paycheck to charity) and stuffing pillowcases with fresh fruit in the Freshman Union to distribute in Harvard Square. I couldn't find it in myself to wish anyone ill. My body throbbed with the presence of Christ.

Over time, though, I realized that I'd never made peace with the teachings of the Church. The Church was the place where I had encountered God, but I didn't know it all that well, in retrospect. I'd spent my intellectual energy reading European philosophy and anti-Mormon literature. I'd never trained my mind on the gospel itself. Some painful but predictable collisions between my learning and my faith awaited me.

I remember still the smothering sensation I felt when I discovered something rather like Lehi's dream of the tree of life in Lucy Mack Smith's family history. My immediate response was to see this as evidence that her son Joseph Smith had plagiarized rather than revealed the Book of Mormon. I see now that I was in over my head, without a clue about the history of the Book of Mormon, Lucy Mack Smith's memoir, the dynamics of memory, or the nature of scripture. The Book of Mormon for me was the still mostly unread book that served as a symbol of my conversion. I hadn't engaged it as a text with an actual history. I hadn't allowed it to be a scripture, in all the dimensions appropriate to such texts. This undergraduate crisis points out another principle: *the framing is often more important than the question.*

In this case I had a simplistic understanding of scripture: I assumed that if there were any hint before 1829 of material that appeared in the Book of Mormon, then the book wasn't scripture. I didn't realize then that my framing required nonsensical assumptions about the nature of scripture. As it happened, I later discovered at least three reasonable explanations. First, Lucy Mack Smith's memory was faulty, and she had written parts of the Book of Mormon into her memoir as part of her attempt to shore up her family's prominence in 1845 Nauvoo. Second, God could easily have prepared the entire Smith family as vessels for the revelation of the Book of Mormon. Third, scripture may in fact be a dialogue between God and the prophets that draws on all participants. The translator of scripture may thus communicate resonances in the present for the scriptures that hope to whisper from the dust.

The problem with getting the framing wrong is common in both religion and science. The way we structure problems drives the conclusions we make, but we often don't notice. And then we get lost, quickly and dangerously. A classic story from clinical cardiology is a cautionary tale in medicine—everyone knew that after heart attacks people sometimes died from dangerous heart rhythms. So researchers asked, "How do we suppress bad rhythms after a heart attack?" Scientists developed medications to do it, clinical researchers studied them, and it was proved that they did in fact decrease the bad rhythms. And then in a large trial, researchers showed that using medications to suppress those rhythms caused more deaths because eliminating one sort of rhythm opened up the heart to other, more lethal alternatives.[2] In retrospect, the field was asking the wrong question. The right questions would require more time and work to define. In honesty, researchers still aren't sure what the right question is for bad rhythms after a heart attack.

On a similar note, we, in my main field of intensive care, once believed that the goal in using the mechanical ventilator or "respirator" was to achieve normal oxygen and carbon dioxide levels in the blood. But then researchers followed an intuition that pushing lungs too hard might be dangerous. In a large study, they showed that the pursuit of normal blood gas levels killed patients. When doctors ran the ventilators the right way, not pushing too hard, patients had lower oxygen and higher carbon dioxide, the opposite of what we thought we should shoot for. Ironically, making patients look worse was the secret to saving their lives.[3] These kinds of errors happen constantly in medicine and science.

Religion isn't free from framing errors, either. Think for a moment about possible views of the Church, as one example among many. If we frame religion as a social club or an instrument for our satisfaction, we will ask whether church attendance is fun every week and makes us feel good about ourselves. Such pleasures are worth treasuring when we find them, to be sure, but they are beside the point. They aren't

---

2. D.S. Echt et al, "Mortality and Morbidity in Patients Receiving Encainide, Flecainide, or Placebo," *New England Journal of Medicine* 324, no. 12 (1991): 781–88.

3. The Acute Respiratory Distress Syndrome Network, "Ventilation with Lower Tidal Volumes as Compared with Traditional Tidal Volumes for Acute Lung Injury and the Acute Respiratory Distress Syndrome," *New England Journal of Medicine* 342, no. 18 (2000): 1301–8.

why the Church exists. Among other important reasons, the Church exists to bring heaven and earth together and to build family communities that extend beyond biology. Similarly, when we imagine that God is a scientific hypothesis to be tested, we can tie ourselves in logical knots and still never see the God who hovers just beyond our capacity to see. Whether we think science "proves" or "disproves" God, if we treat God as a scientific hypothesis, we will never have a clue about the lives of our Heavenly Parents. *The framing is often more important than the question.*

3. *I need to allow myself to be wrong.*

I finished my freshman year tentative about the Church. I believed in God, and I trusted God to direct me away from a full-time mission if I wasn't supposed to go. God didn't tell me not to, so I continued down the path God and I had outlined right after my conversion. Following difficult encounters with the temple and then the Missionary Training Center, I ended up in the hot, wet poverty of southern Louisiana, bewildered by mission life. Something in me snapped after a few months. I became rigid, humorless, and judgmental. I tried to skip preparation day so that I could spend more time proselytizing. I became certain about how other people needed to be and tried to mold them to my vision. In my defense, I was as ruthless in judgment of myself as I was of others, but that didn't lessen the brutality. I lived the holy misery of a scrupulous perfectionist deep in the mission field. I needed to learn another principle: *I had to let myself be wrong.*

The capacity to admit when we are wrong is a crucial trait in religion and science. Here I want to focus on religion: Christian humility urges us to see ourselves and others as God sees us, simultaneously glorious and never as wise as we think. When I hear President Uchtdorf encourage us to "doubt our doubts," he is in part urging on us the patient humility that is required for all learning. My own experience has been that rigid arrogance is equally a temptation in religion and science, among theists and atheists alike. The gentle patience that comes with humility has allowed me to take my time in pondering hard questions. I'm not talking about moral relativism here. I see moral relativism as a way of abandoning the pursuits that bring life its substance and meaning. Instead I'm wanting to be aware that we are all making our way toward truth. That journey will last much longer than our mortal lives, but it's a journey that brings to mortality its power and beauty. The way forward is the humble pursuit of truth.

Allowing ourselves to be wrong also means that we must cut ourselves a little slack. We will not get everything right the first time. We cannot live without imperfection. Only God is perfect. We will try and fail, and we will try and fail again. That is the mortal experiment: to try and fail in the community of our Heavenly Parents and their human children.

4. We belong to each other.

After my mission I settled back into undergraduate life. I was committed to the Church and slowly mellowed a little. I found myself in a bishopric and discovered a new kind of stress, related to discovering people's dependence on me. More than one student in the ward told me that, in the pressurized world of academic skeptics we inhabited in Boston, they reassured themselves that if Sam Brown believed, then they could believe too. Those compliments, if that's what they were, shook me to the core. I was too aware of how hard it was for me to believe, how unnatural it all was. I couldn't bear the thought of being responsible for another person's unhappiness, let alone their capacity to trust God. I was glad to be released from the bishopric when I graduated college, too old to continue in the university ward. I was eager to be free of the weight of others' need.

I felt called to stay in Boston for medical school, although I thought Baltimore sounded more interesting. I met my wife that summer after college, commencing the most important relationship of my life. The mountains called to me more than church meetings, and she was a good sport, accompanying me into New Hampshire's White Mountains. I scheduled as many weekend camping trips as I could. At the time I thought I was just pursuing my passions for wilderness. I see now that I was running from another important principle—*we belong to each other*.

It took me years to understand how deep my fear of belonging ran. I saw in retrospect that I had been skipping church so that I wouldn't have to face the people I worshiped with. I felt overwhelmed by their need for me to be better than I was. I don't mean that they were judgmental: they were just the opposite. But I felt their anxious need and couldn't shake the feeling that I owed them succor. I couldn't bear the intensity of it. A similar fear of having people depend on me delayed parenthood for years after our marriage. I see now that this fear stunted my growth personally and even spiritually. I needed to feel deep down in my soul that whether we like it or not, we depend on each other. This dependence is a fixed fact about the universe; I couldn't deny it any more than I could deny that the moon glows when the sun has ducked beneath the horizon and the earth does not stand between the two of them.

I wonder now whether this anxiety about mattering to other people was a flight from my father's memory. His deformed life twisted above me like the sharp sword above the nervous Damocles of Greek tradition. But in the straining toward God that my wife and others guided, I finally saw that the old story I told about myself as unable to bear the weight of others' needs wasn't good enough. It wasn't true, and it wasn't courageous. Recognizing that others' burdens were my burdens too allowed me to see that if they needed something from me, then I could rise to the occasion. I couldn't live in my own little world because I had to live in the real one, where people depend on each other.

At a practical level, this awareness of human interdependence slowly began to shape my behaviors. I became less prone to grandstanding, less inclined to expect that people would bend their needs to my personal preferences. I stopped making partisan political statements at church, and I tried to pay closer attention to the emotional needs of my scientific collaborators. I'm still not great at it, but this work of bearing and sharing burdens and love will last my entire life.

5. I am not the smartest or best person in the room.

In our early thirties, my wife and I began to ask hard questions about how and where we wanted to raise our daughters and what we wanted the middle stretches of our lives to look like. We realized, acutely, that we missed the mountains. For a variety of reasons we didn't entirely understand, we decided to return to Salt Lake City. I immediately regretted the decision. I saw myself as an East Coast intellectual and assumed that I could only be a practicing Latter-day Saint in Boston. I bought into the stories people like to tell about "Utah Mormons" and believed that I would never fit in. At the time I didn't see my arrogance for what it was because it was different from the rigidity of my mission. Seeing this arrogance took time and distance. I had to learn another principle: *I am not the smartest or best person in the room.*

Erik Erikson was, for decades, a world-famous psychoanalyst of young people. He invented the concept of the "identity crisis" and was often introduced as the best psychoanalyst since Freud. If the stories are true, Professor Erikson couldn't bear the compliment because being the greatest living psychoanalyst wasn't good enough for him. He hadn't beaten Freud. His insecurity was so severe that his daughter Sue wrote a bitter memoir after he died, detailing his failings as a father.[4] I'm haunted by Sue's complaints because I realize how much my

---

4.   Sue Erikson Bloland, *In the Shadow of Fame: A Memoir by the Daughter of Erik H. Erikson* (New York: Viking, 2005).

sinful desire to be the smartest person in the room has been both predictable and destructive.

I've had to work at it. I've had to swallow my pride. In a word, I've needed to imagine myself as God sees me rather than the way I wish my peers and competitors would see me.

There are two aspects to this idea that we shouldn't be the best person in the room. First, as far as possible, we should try to surround ourselves with people who are smarter and better than we are because they have things to teach us. Second and more importantly, we have to make a choice to see the world anew. We must discover in others what is beautiful and gracious and wise. In any room, we will encounter people who are better than we are. This can be hard work, especially if you've spent your life being complimented for how smart or successful or ambitious you are. But it's necessary to the life of Christ.

6. *Love well and often.*

My wife and I found Utah a marvelous place, full of good, wise, kind people. We chose to treat our ward members and neighbors with love, and they loved us back. Life entered its middle phases. I let myself churn the way the world wants us to churn, like so much overwhipped butter. Physician scientists have a way of working constantly, seeing patients, training the next generation of doctors, writing grants, attending conferences and committee meetings, doing the actual science, and writing up the results. I was, in the vacuous and overburdened adjective of our age, "busy."

Life changed again when we turned forty. This time the change came through tragedy, with a cancer in the family. This heartbreak pushed me from my cerebral, professional approach to life and forced me to become open to other ways of knowing and being.

My wife and I rebuilt our lives in the aftermath of that illness. I found myself working less and spending more time as an equal partner in our marriage. I'd found a comfortable place intellectually in terms of my testimony, but I had huge gaps in my spiritual life. I realized more than ever before that faith was about more than mastering the doctrines of the Restoration. Faith was about learning to love. I would need to *love well and often.*

I began to spend more time with our elderly neighbors, cooked dinner for strangers, and started baking cookies for church. I tried to listen to the stories people tell and compliment them more. I worked to love strangers. I felt the spirit of Christ calling me to love. I was a novice, but I felt my heart softening. Our contemporary culture tells us that people should seek their own bliss and not get too involved in the lives of others. It's better to have a good job, a nice place to live, and fulfilling hobbies than do the strenuous work of community. But the gospel tells us that we are nothing without other people and that the measure of our lives is how richly we have loved. The culture warriors tell us that our opponents are incomprehensible and unforgivable, their sins so outrageous that they fall beyond our obligation to love them. But the gospel tells us that we are to love well and often—even, especially, our opponents. That is the chilling message at the crux of the Sermon on the Mount in Matthew 5:43–48.

In love I find myself educated and reshaped. In love I find myself enlightened. It's not just that faith—understood as believing true things—requires the work to actually understand the doctrines involved. It's that the work of loving, well and often, is necessary to faith and knowledge. Without that love we will create destructive versions of science, religion, and society. Without that love we cannot know what it means to live. Without that love we cannot know God.

These principles and experiences have brought me to where I stand today. I'm aware that *what's missing is often what's most important* and *the framing is often more important than the question.* I'm working to *let myself be wrong* and to *know that I'm not the smartest person in the room.* And I'm struggling with all my energy to feel deeply that *we belong to each other* and to *love well and often.*

I'm a scientist and a scholar who loves a good argument and a difficult puzzle to solve. I find the methods of science effective and inspiring, even if they're not the whole story. And I'm a believer who is learning the meanings of life that love discloses. I'm slowly discovering a little more about God, much of which is in experience rather than mere facts. I've become acutely aware of just how funny life is.

Life is marvelously, deliciously strange. And in that strangeness stands a saving mystery.

Nowadays we like to think about the world as orderly and predictable. There are a few rules of physics that cover astronomy and geology, DNA takes care of biology, and butterflies flapping their wings in Brazil take care of the weather. These ideas about order in nature have helped us to build marvelous machines to manipulate our worlds and to make astonishing strides in medicine. Some people love this notion of rules so much that they imagine that we human beings are merely machines—robots in suits of flesh, automatically acting out the inherent rules that govern atoms and electricity.

This modern, mechanical view of the world is tempting. Life feels easier when we imagine that it's perfectly predictable and controllable. There's just one problem with this view of the world: it requires that we pretend that the tip is the entire iceberg, that the oceans are just a wet road we drive boats on.

This simplistic story isn't even true for science. We have dark matter, quantum uncertainties, the coiled dimensions of string theory, and the bizarre menagerie of subatomic particles. Scientists, even the nominally atheist ones, aren't afraid to exclaim at the vast beauty of the universe and its constituents. The best scientists have left themselves the capacity to be surprised, even gloriously so, by their subjects of study.

But then I have to wonder. If we're okay with the world being funny when the scientists notice its delicious strangeness, why can't we let the world be funny in other ways? We seem to be happy with quarks and bosons and particles that wander backwards in time. Why shouldn't we be just as happy with the possibility that human consciousness persists after death in the presence of God? Why shouldn't we allow the possibility that the true Light of Christ is a sacred force in which we all live and breathe and have our being?[5]

When we lose our capacity to see the world in its true strangeness, we lose our ability to see beneath the surface of the ocean. We sail blind.

The view of the world as merely physical is a common and notorious one. And we need to admit to ourselves that experimental science has brought us many wonderful things. It is not all wrong—far from it—even if it is fundamentally incomplete.

What we believers need now, I think, is the capacity to see above and below the surface of the sea. We need to be able to see both what is temporary and physical and what is eternal and spiritual. We will need to learn, in the language of the legal scholar Jeremy Waldron, to "scintillate."[6] It's an odd word that captures both the flickering quality of bouncing back and forth between the two ways of seeing and some of

---

5.   John Durham Peters has helped me think through these ideas. I pursue these ideas in greater detail in "The (True) Light of Christ in Joseph Smith's Revelations," in *How and What You Worship: Christology and Praxis in the Revelations of Joseph Smith*, ed. Rachel Cope, Carter Charles, and Jordan T. Watkins (Provo, UT: Religious Studies Center, Brigham Young University; Salt Lake City: Deseret Book, 2020), 99–122.

6.   Jeremy Waldron, *One Another's Equals: The Basis of Human Equality* (Cambridge, MA: Harvard University Press, 2017), esp. 156–57, 207.

the excitement of this process. We as Latter-day Saints could stand to learn better to scintillate between the earthly and the heavenly, the secular and the religious, the immanent and the transcendent. We could stand to know and love and live the present life of the world and also to know and love and live the celestial world. We belong to them both.

This interdependence of temporal and spiritual is one of the defining attributes of the restored gospel. The temporal and the spiritual cannot ultimately be separated. In Doctrine and Covenants 29, God revisits the creation of Eve and Adam while explaining the nature of beginnings and endings. In verse 34, God announces, "I say unto you that all things unto me are spiritual, and not at any time have I given unto you a law which was temporal." Dozens of other scriptures say the same thing. A strict separation of the two realms is impossible.

The work of scintillation, of flickering back and forth between the two worlds, is tiring. It requires careful attention and devotion. Many of our friends and family may fear motion sickness, preferring to see the temporal as "all there is." Since we can do technology and a lot of science without looking under the water's surface, we'd rather just train our eyes on the horizon and forget about the world beneath the water. But by doing so, we are cutting off our nose to spite our face. Refusing to see the spiritual beside the temporal is like staging an opera in mime. Not that you can't have creative and interesting performance art with a stage full of mimes, but it would be a parody of opera. No sound, no opera. Or, to step back from opera to a more accessible analogy, systematically excluding the spiritual from view is like trying to fly without wings.

But we are called to dance, with body and soul. God calls us to see the divine face in other people, to sense God's spirit in the natural world. Our Heavenly Parents call us to scintillate with them in the eternal dance that transfigures our eternal souls through the continuous work of faith.

Lost in Identity

Twice I was mistaken for a homeless man my freshman year of college. One occasion I saw as funny; the other seared me.

I started college as a free spirit, an anti-authority atheist who had just got religion. I still walked and talked like a Utah country boy aspiring to be a hippie, but I was newly Christian. I prayed, often, to know who I was under these new rules of the game of life. I made myself open to new relationships. My friendships within Boston's homeless community helped to define me in that period of change.

At the same time, college was good to me. Nothing seemed too pressing, and not even unimportant problems intruded on the early morning. I often shuffled to the Freshman Union in search of a buffet breakfast, paid for by the donations of rich dead men, well after nine o'clock.

I staggered out of my room one morning, wearing a green polyester sweater with more holes than hems, and a pair of equally ramshackle jeans. I think I was wearing the rope-soled espadrilles I'd appropriated from a high school girlfriend, the footwear not much thicker than my callused soles. My shoulder-length blond hair, washed daily but unacquainted with comb or brush, streamed lazily about my face. Sometimes it caught in the stubble I could be bothered to shave perhaps once a week. Harvard Yard was nearly empty, and it dawned on me that the college was on vacation and the Freshman Union was closing tomorrow, which was, I thought, maybe Sunday? Without the money to travel, I wasn't as skilled as my schoolmates at tracking vacation schedules.

Content to wander, oblivious, along the paved path through the elm-shrouded yard, I made my way to breakfast. Lost in the pleasure of solitude, I almost collided with a middle-aged woman with a shopping bag and unseasonably thick clothing. Her frame was a comfortable cross between obesity and grandmotherly hospitality. Her face had seen too much sun. The wrinkles and rough spots reminded me of the future of my own fair skin, and I winced.

"Sorry," I muttered. I hoped I was friendly.

"No problem. How's it going? No one's here."

"Yeah, I was just wondering about that. I think it's a vacation or something. Great weather though."

I touched her upper arm, indicating a desire to continue on my way. We resumed an easy pace together, passing the red brick box that served as an undergraduate library in the shadow of the stately Widener Library.

"You bet. Can't complain. You from around here?"

"Not really. I've been here for a few months. Before that I was from Utah. I miss the mountains, but I like Boston too. I'm not really a city guy."

She smiled, a little. "I grew up in Philly. I've never been in the mountains. I just got here. So far, so good, I guess."

"It grows on you. What brings you to Cambridge?" I asked, uncertain how to place her, whether absentminded professor, concerned college parent, or tourist.

"Just trying out a new city. So how is it here?"

"Nice overall, if you're a city person."

"But I mean, you know, people. Are they generous?"

"I don't know. They're a little colder than back west, but not too bad."

"How much do you get in a day? Is it enough to live on?"

"I guess they treat me solid here," I replied, not wanting to explain the intricacies of needs-blind admission and needs-based scholarships. I had won that jackpot and was still a bit muddled about how to describe the transition from kid on church welfare to scholarship student at an Ivy League college.

"Where are the best places to go?"

"Huh?" I let slip, slowly appreciating that we were chatting at cross-purposes.

"For money, you know, panhandling. You said they treat you solid here."

I laughed, hoping not to offend. "I'm sorry, I misunderstood. I don't panhandle. I'm a student here. I don't have any cash, but you've gotta join me for breakfast."

After awkward smiles, she allowed me to be a mess with a home, and I allowed her to be one without. She refused to join me in the cafeteria but agreed that I could smuggle her some food from the buffet. I came back out with fruit and pastries. She escaped to a more straightforward world where homeless means homeless and Harvard means Harvard. I forgot to ask her name.

The second time I was mistaken for a homeless man, later that school year, wasn't funny. Not at all.

AG and I were casual friends. Most weeks, as I passed from my academic cloister to the bustle of Harvard Square, he sat beside the Unitarian Church, all smiles but few teeth, black leather boots with a glued-on ankle chain. His tan fedora was smooth and stiff with accumulated sweat and dust. He usually held an old guitar, little more than an overweight ukulele. Sometimes he would strum and sing, his rough voice searching for notes while his eyes reached for attention. I sometimes stopped and listened, mesmerized by the rough rustling of his eroded vocal cords. Sometimes we spoke.

We didn't talk about where we came from or where we went. He did not know I slept in a warm room just a few hundred yards away, and I did not ask which shelter he used or whether he maybe even had private housing. I never asked what AG stood for. We knew that we were both free somehow, and that was enough. Sometimes we talked about the weather or wondered about music and outer space, basketball and politics. Mostly we recognized each other's existence.

Once, in spring, I approached the intersection of streets where he worked and found him delighting with his nose and eyes in a daisy in a waxed paper cup. The flower had seen better days—mashed leaves in dingy white threaded to a solid green stalk. But it was thirsty, AG informed me. Would I watch his studio while he sneaked into a convenience store bathroom for some tap water? I acquiesced: I was early to work and had thirty minutes free. Happily, almost greedily, AG acknowledged my help and rushed down Massachusetts Avenue.

I lay my book bag down next to his dirty black duffel, his ukulele resting against it. To its side lay a wire-bound notebook. I scanned the open page. Some scratches were a musical notation—curved staves and spider legs. Other markings were unrecognizable words sown by a quivering pen. I could not interpret the glyphs, but I was pretty sure they were song lyrics.

When I looked up from the notebook, I felt suddenly outside the flow of the world. It seemed ominous, like the first wild moments of an unexpected snowstorm above timberline, as the visibility drops toward zero. I scanned the faces of passersby to see whether they sensed what I did. I found my answer in their faces, twisting as if they were squinting with their shoulders. I suspect they had no knowledge of or intent to follow the choreography that seemed to me to guide their movements. Each tensing of the back, every missed step and hurried pace told me that I was intruding, that I did not belong in the human family. No one stepped on me or stumbled over me, preferring to trip against the rough edges of stray bricks.

Directionless anger and pain scalded my temples and cheeks. I strained to catch my existence the way old men struggle to catch their breath. For what seemed thirty minutes, I searched the throng for some proof that I belonged. I tried to be rational, to remember that Boston isn't the West. People don't greet each other in big cities. And our worth as human beings isn't a function of whether people acknowledge us. There's more to us than popularity. But this was deeper. Before, when I was in college, people did not greet me, but they recognized me. Even in our Northeastern hurry, we knew each other, felt unconsciously a shared identity. Now, I believed, they did not know me. Or would not. And that introduced me to a severe vulnerability. I hadn't expected such painful empathy with AG, but there I was.

I was ashamed of my worn clothing, of my long, knotted hair and stubbled cheeks and chin. I felt disconnected from grades and scholarships. I decayed and I ached. This was as close as I'd come in adulthood to the feeling of annihilation, that vague and sometimes vivid specter of adolescence for many of us who are prone to fits of melancholy.

I don't know how long I sat that way, lost in shame. AG did finally return, his small, sparkling eyes above his chafed, ruddy cheeks. He held his treasured flower tightly. The daisy was no comelier than before, but it was bathed and fed.

I relinquished the throne to the returning king. "Thanks," AG offered, his attention absorbed, like his water, by the hungry roots of this new love. I mumbled something like "No problem," too uncertain of myself to say more. I fled back to the world where I belonged and mattered.

I told those stories from time to time to friends and ward members—the experience settled in my soul and taught me something about Christ's ministry, both during his lifetime and during mine. The stories changed over time in the retelling, especially as they came filtered through others' minds. There was a funny story: a homeless woman asked for panhandling advice because I was a disheveled hippie. And there was a sad story: I experienced the casual denial of my humanity as I sat among a homeless man's belongings. Within a couple of years, the two experiences had merged in the lore of our ward. Rumor had it that everybody—homeless and otherwise—thought I was homeless, and I'd made a stack of money by panhandling when I watched AG's stuff that day. I don't doubt that AG sometimes made a little money busking in front of the Unitarian Church, but no one dropped even a coin while I was watching his space. The first time I heard the new, cheerfully merged story, I felt stung by the memory. Although I knew perfectly well how stories change over time—that change is as natural as speech—I still bore the imprint of that half hour on the sidewalk.

Sometimes I'd like to have the story be different. If I made money from the experience, it would be funny, even warmhearted. But the real story was a desperate and hard one. The way my friends remembered the stories is not so different from the way many of us read the New Testament. We want that old scripture to be a lovely story about how we get to heaven. But more often it's about how blind we are to the suffering of those at the margins. It is often more convicting than comforting, so we hold it at arm's length.

I also think that something about identity is at stake in these stories. These were experiences of lost identity, misplaced position. In the funny story, I was in control: I had a breakfast to share and residential security to parade. The homeless woman was powerless and therefore no threat to my identity, so my friends and I could laugh. *How funny that you were unkempt back then.*

In the painful story, *I* was powerless, unable to make the world see me. Those who looked past me had carefully secured identities—they were students, police officers, salespeople, and professional academics. Their threat to my significance felt painfully real. I was bereft of the supports of identity I had come to require. In the composite story, my identity was safe, and I profited from the mistaken identity. There was no pain, only material advantage. And we all know when we hear it how safe I must have felt, making money hand over fist.

My friends know, I think instinctively, that their identity is as fragile as mine. We too often depend on our position, our access to or exercise of power to place us in the world. Many of us have spent years, if not decades, building careers to keep us safe and secure. But if our context were misplaced, we would be existential leaves tumbling before an autumn wind. That instability hurts; sometimes it burns. But maybe that kind of awareness, that floating between worldly identity and the reality of human interdependence, is what Jesus calls us to. He never told anyone to sit complacent in their worldly identity. Instead Jesus invites us, "Come, take up the cross, and follow me" (Mark 10:21). Jacob invites us to "bear the shame of the world" (Jacob 1:8). God asks us to lose the easy lives our society has constructed. These are hard words, and I have struggled all of my adulthood to heed the call. My failings, our failings, aren't the whole story, though. Wherever and whoever we are, we are called to follow Jesus into the quiet mingling among the vulnerable and forgotten, sharing their identity. This is hard work, but it belongs to God.

This belonging to God has always been tricky for me, the same way my experience with homelessness was bittersweet. There's something exciting, even fun, about life with God. Such pleasure or relief is what we as believers tend to emphasize when we talk about religion. But it's not as simple as that.

There's also something painful at play. The ancient Hebrews worried that if they came too immediately into the presence of God they would be burned up: people could be incinerated by even an inappropriate hand on the ark of covenant, like poor, infamous Uzzah (see 2 Samuel 6). Even forgetting that threat of immolation, direct contact with God can be painful, not because God is cruel, but because godliness means loving those who suffer and seeing the world clearly.

We've cherished as Latter-day Saints the image in Moses 7 of God weeping with Enoch as God surveys the world before the Flood. There's even the playful and heart-wrenching metaphor that the waters of the Flood were God and Creation weeping together. But we often forget that Enoch shed tears as well. At the end of the passage (Moses 7:41), Enoch too participates in the life of God so thoroughly that he weeps as he looks at the world that he and his people of Zion have just left. He had been translated; he was able to bear the direct presence of God. And even so, the love in that presence has brought him sadness. Enoch found that identifying closely with other human beings through Christ has brought terrible sadness because those beloved people suffer and cause suffering. That's the risk of love and the associated risk of identity. Moses 7 is at once hopeful and defiant. This passage is saying that we don't understand the way the world works. Jesus's love isn't just in the heart, it's also in the mind. This love teaches us how the world works, and it is both glorious and sad. God's love is all we need, yet it is more than we can bear. There will be laughter and tears, comfort and discomfort. The familiar stories won't make the same kind of sense anymore. We're going to see the world differently.

There's a hymn we as a people have loved since Joseph Smith's time. Back then it was called "The Stranger," but we know it best by its opening line, "A Poor Wayfaring Man of Grief." Each verse contains another version of the same story: a struggling stranger encounters the narrator, who responds in kindness. The stranger is starving or in prison or physically wounded, and the narrator works to heal the wounds. Finally the stranger "start[s] from disguise" and reveals himself as the risen Christ, bearing the marks of the Crucifixion. At the level where I've always understood it, this hymn is telling a simple and familiar story about our need to care for the suffering stranger. Being a good person means loving other people, which in turn means loving Jesus. That's entirely true from the perspective of the narrator. But what if the hymn is a story about Jesus and other homeless people? What if it's telling us about their shared identity, reconciling us to each other and all of us to Christ? What if we're asked to be open to true, shared identity? And what if that flowing of identity stands at the center of atonement?

We've all heard and said the platitudes about walking in someone else's shoes for a mile. That's important. Empathy is an important life skill. But we're also called to something higher and harder: to try to inhabit others and allow them to inhabit us, to share their joy and their pain. It's unnerving and overwhelming. I can see why my friends weren't sure what to make of my experiences as a fake homeless man.

I don't want to be grandiose here; that's the opposite of what I mean. The idea is not to be grand, but to be common. These run-ins I had with homelessness and the people it afflicts are my own encounter with the most sacred story of a homeless man we know: the New Testament. Jesus began life as a carpenter's son but once the time for his mission had arrived, he became a homeless prophet. We think of his life as adventurous, but he was poor and had nowhere to call home. His life was not glamorous. When a possible disciple approached him, eager to follow the miracle-working prophet, Jesus replied, "Foxes have dens, and the birds of the sky have nests, but the Son of Man has nowhere to lay his head" (Luke 9:58 and Matthew 8:20, author's translation). Jesus was throwing water on the fire of this man's ardor, reminding him that identification with the Messiah is not cozy or easy or even reassuring. I think I have a sense for what that prospective disciple might have felt, lessons learned in part from my own tangled identities with homelessness when I was in college. That is what God does: God disorients us to reconcile us in one.

In Praise of the Inauthentic Life

What a lousy bunch of conformists, I thought. *Bleeping sheep.* In such aggressive stereotypes, I dismissed the main body of Latter-day Saints among whom I was staggering through a dissipated adolescence in Davis County, Utah. To my eye, Church members had only enough wits to look the same, follow their prophets, and regurgitate their dogmas. There wasn't a free thinker among them as far as I was concerned. I, on the other hand, was perfectly free. No one could constrain me, however hard they might try.

I understood my cultural situation in terms of a test of loyalty that sometimes circulated at the time. Serious Church members in our community occasionally posed a rhetorical question as a proof of their commitment: "If the prophet tells you to jump, do you ask how high?" The answer was supposed to be yes, but my answer to that test oath was, roughly, to figure out what the opposite of jumping was, film myself anti-jumping, and then send the prophet a videotape of my performance. I was no follower.

I saw myself then as a lone wolf who could see the rotten core of religious community. That self-image was the beating heart of my identity. I had reasons for what I did and the way I thought about human community. Bad food, a broken home, and tattered clothing told me that the world was cruel and that I did not matter. Misery had driven me away from God. I resented the absence in my life of a functional father; I felt his abdication of parental responsibilities every day of my childhood. At a personal level, I was fat and clumsy, unable to participate usefully in sports. I was bookish instead, uncomfortable in social situations.

I defied as many of the community norms as I could: what to say, what to wear, how to go to school, what to believe. In high school, I occasionally encountered violent resistance to my protest. Although I wondered whether I was gay for only a year or two, I violated gender expectations with my haircut and dress as a New Waver. So the cowboys and rockers yelled "faggot" in my direction and occasionally punched me or shoved me into lockers. I remember one night in our kitchen tearfully recounting my frightened hatred for the bullies to my mother. I should be clear: I never suffered anything physical beyond temporary bruises. But I remember being attacked for being different. It was terrible.

I experienced my alienation as evidence that no one understood me. Communities rejected me, and I rejected them back. The image of myself as the never-understood outsider took much longer to leave me than my atheism did. Wandering out of my do-it-yourself French existentialism, I abandoned the atheism of Albert Camus long before I could part ways with the image of his alienated man killing an Arab, or the philosopher-writer himself wrapping stiff lips around a half-burnt cigarette.[1] As many another defiant soul, I had little

---

1.   The image of the slain Arab is from his 1942 *The Stranger*.

idea then how much I was acting out an established script. Discovering that script and its history took decades.

From my alienated perch, I was blind to the goodness of the communities in which I lived and breathed and had my being. When the police came one night to issue an arrest warrant against my father for writing bad checks, the ward was prepared to help. Church members brought us food from their gardens. When I needed a car to get to work at a fast food restaurant one town over, neighbors sold me a car for one dollar and then, when that car inevitably died, they replaced it with a van. Men in the ward took me camping, introducing me to a feral world that made the image of God conceivable to me. Those blind-faith Latter-day Saints did a lot of listening to and loving of this boy who worked to defy them at every turn. That ward held our family in its bosom. I attacked and resented, and they loved in response. We were not all alike in the Kaysville Fifth Ward, far from it, but we were family.

In addition to the older ward members who looked out for my family, I was fortunate to have close friends who were decent people less confused than I was. While they didn't always know what to do with me, these teens loved me and were glad to spend time together. They provided a community that grew rapidly in the aftermath of my conversion to theism.

While I made a public transition to belief in a testimony meeting in August 1990, several of my friends weren't present that Sunday morning. About a week later, a group of us went camping in the Wasatch Mountains above our homes. A rain settled in after sunset, when we had stuffed our bodies and sleeping bags into a large tent. Several of them asked me to share the Spirit I had encountered during the sacrament prayer earlier that month. I thought I could. Why not? I was young enough to think that God would do what I asked when I asked it. We gathered in a circle on our knees, facing the center of the tent. I don't remember whether we held hands, but it felt like we had. We each prayed aloud, one after the other. I don't remember the words any of us spoke together in that dark tent. In my memory, our prayers have merged with the insistent knocking of raindrops on nylon. The enveloping rain fell from the sky in syncopated waves. I added my voice to the song the sky sang with the fabric of our tent. Spirit, world, and the bonds of friendship circled tight around my heart. We wept together in God's presence.

We remain friends to this day. I've been told that these relationships we still enjoy thirty years later are deeper than we have any right to expect from high school friendships. I don't know why that community has persisted, although it is a gracious gift that I treasure. I suspect that our shared experience of spiritual transformation had a role to play in this endurance. Those bonds are strong. They will last an eternity.

Even after my conversion, I continued uncertain how to inhabit a community. I took books to parties so that I could read quietly in the kitchen rather than learn small talk. When the time came, I wasn't the husband or father I could have been, too occupied with my own concerns. Even though I attended church regularly, I refused visits from home teachers because I didn't want to be bothered. I tended to grandstand at church, making sure people heard my politics and knew that I was no "blind-faith" believer. I was not going to be dominated by what someone else wanted from me. Even as I continued steadfast in my basic belief in God, I was skeptical of any authority that another person, let alone a community, might exert over me. My whole life has been defiant; it is my natural state.

Then my wife got sick, and I looked harder than I ever had at the nature of identity and community. The experience changed me. I became more committed at home and more patient with difference at church. I finally managed to think less about myself than I did about others. I began to taste in a consistent way the bittersweet, transformative tang of humility.

I saw all aspects of my life differently in the white-hot light of repentance. I realized that my resistance to the demands of community had interfered with my ability to do right by my patients. I had been afraid to allow the bonds of community to exist with my patients and their families. I had preferred the social and emotional distance that came from hiding in the pack of doctors that circulates in the intensive care units. Emboldened by the love of my wife and the power of new-found humility, I worked to create connections with the people I met in the hospital. I've discovered that, professionally, the work that matters most to me as a person and that has the most positive impact in the broader world is the capacity to understand patients and families as equal. In retrospect, my resistance to community was affecting not just my Church participation but all aspects of my life.

The transition into the bonds of community in adulthood has been strange and uncomfortable. My new life is deeply inauthentic when judged by my past. But this defiant outsider has learned how to participate in community and discover identity there. From this new vantage point the world looks different.

To see the way I now do, I had to break free from certain modern ideologies whose hold on me I had not appreciated, let alone understood. As I explore the nature of identity in the modern world, I want to flag important questions at the out-set. As I think about the importance of a life centered in the love and service of others, some Saints may wonder how their life experiences might fit into such a world. Their concerns matter.

First, some have already heeded Christ's call to service so profoundly that they are worn to the bone—exhausted, depressed, and anxious. I pray that they know they are well loved and can find rest among us. They are good and faith-ful servants. There is rest for them, both now and hereafter. I hope that those of us who are lazier will look for ways to ease the burdens of the exhausted. When I talk about identity and selflessness, I'm hoping to find balance. For someone who is already selfless, calls to selflessness should be ignored.

Second, some among us have suffered abuse. Alongside other terrible consequences, the sin of abuse corrupts the community that could otherwise offer protection and healing. Abuse is an evil that we must prevent and protest whenever we can. It's my prayer that understanding these topics clearly will alert the rest of us to the need to support those who have been abused or are currently being abused. My heart aches for those who suffer. I pray that understanding modern identity better will help us to love better and more thoroughly those who struggle in pain. If we who have not been abused are too busy with our own self-fashioning, we will have little capacity to carry the love of Christ to those who suffer.

These disclaimers are necessary and important; we ignore them at our peril. With the needs of the vulnerable in mind, we should explore the contours of our modern cultural plight.

The cultural changes that affect us the most began several centuries ago but have intensified sharply over the last few decades.[2] One of the most important is that we in the West increasingly look inside our heads rather than outside them to know ourselves.[3] This pattern of thought has become so familiar to us now that we're a little bewildered when we try to imagine the old ways. In the past, when people wanted to know who they were, they tended to cast their gaze elsewhere: at the natural world, at God, at the people they loved, at the village where they lived. That's where they located the touch-

2. Here I follow the argument of Charles Taylor, *A Secular Age* (Cambridge: Harvard University Press, 2007). He makes similar, openly religious arguments in his *A Catholic Modernity?* The Protestant theologian James Smith has digested Taylor's arguments into the popular and accessible *How (Not) to Be Secular* (Grand Rapids, MI: Eerdmans, 2014).

3. Matthew Crawford, *The World Beyond Your Head* (New York: FSG, 2014) provides a complementary approach to Taylor's.

stone of their identity, the places where they discovered the meanings of their lives.

Not anymore. That's not where identity and meaning come from today, for a hundred different reasons. Some of these reasons feel inevitable, like the relentless moving for school and work. Others feel more contingent, even accidental, like the stories we watch and read or the ways we talk about other people. As a consequence of many social and cultural changes, now we look inside ourselves, as if our mind were a deep pool, and our identity were a goldfish swimming below the surface. That magical fish, we are convinced, contains the authentic kernel that will tell us who we really are. In other words, we now seem to imagine that we can find the answer to the meaning of our lives in an empty room with a locked door and no internet connection. People call this "authenticity," and it's closely tied to a culture some call "expressive individualism," in which our primary task in life is to broadcast our authentic identity to the outside world.[4] When I first read scholarly writings on these topics five years ago, I immediately recognized my younger self as having been a true believer in authenticity. In a modern quest to liberate ourselves from constraint—a pursuit often, we ought to acknowledge, driven by righteous impulses—we may unwittingly abandon the true and abiding foundation of identity.

The old ways may feel as bizarre to us now as believing the earth is flat or the sun revolves around it. Or maybe we think older ideas about selves are like the beliefs that drove the occasional brutal excesses of the Spanish Inquisition. We see our compasses as internal now. We and we alone know and control the meaning of our lives. In the notorious phrase of William Henley's poem "Invictus," we are the masters of our fates and the captains of our souls. Others have no credible

---

4.   On "expressive individualism," see, e.g., Robert Bellah et al., *Habits of the Heart: Individualism and Commitment in American Life* (Berkeley: University of California Press, 1985), 32–35.

claim on us. We are free. I know that story well and cherished it for most of my life.

The modern image of human selves as the captains of their own souls is nowhere present in the scriptures. Nothing in the Old Testament imagines people the way we do now. The ancient Hebrews knew themselves by knowing the people they were committed to. They knew themselves through their covenant with Jehovah.

The New Testament was, if anything, clearer that identity came through God and community. In Jesus's ministry even the emphasis on Israelite versus Gentile was absorbed into Christ. The old covenant with Israel had become a new covenant with the entire world. The revelation through Christ proclaimed that our identity both exists through eternity and comes only in our relation with others. This, I believe, is how to understand Christ's prayer to his Heavenly Father in John 17. Christ prays for his followers and their converts, "that they may all be one as thou, Father, art in me, and I in thee, that they also may be one in us." He further explains that "the glory which thou gavest me I have given them, that they may be one, even as we are one" (John 17:21–22). In other words, Jesus called his disciples to know themselves in the faces and hearts of the people they loved, just as he knows himself in their faces.

At times Jesus made this point in scandalous terms: if we want to find our real selves, then we must abandon the quest itself. That's the painful message of Matthew 10:39—they that find their lives shall lose it; and they that lose their lives for his sake shall find it. When the Gospel of John considers a variation on this theme in chapter 12, verse 25, Jesus clarifies that "they that love their lives shall lose them; and they that hate their lives in this world shall keep them unto life eternal." Over the years, people have interpreted these passages in many different ways. Some have caricatured them as suggesting that Christians want us to ignore this world and its problems. Instead of engaging the world, on this interpretation, Christians sit passively in the face of evil, dreaming of the castles they will inherit if only they can live self-righteously ascetic lives to the end.

These caricatured interpretations are wrong because they assume that what Jesus called us to forget was *life*. But that doesn't make any sense, and it's contrary to the gospel. If life doesn't matter, why was Christ made flesh? Why would the divine Son of God enter mortality if there's no point to the world? The Gnostics thought they had an answer, in their peculiar view of Plato's teachings about transcendence. They said that the physical world, including human bodies, was a prison from which their spirits had to escape back to a perfect world of spirits. But Jesus was no Gnostic. Christ became mortal because the world matters. No Christian story of heaven can be told without earth.

The miracle of Christ's entry into mortality, what the Book of Mormon calls his "condescension" (1 Nephi 11:16), was that he came to life *for others*. He was the perfect son of perfect parents, chosen as the linchpin of the plan for our salvation. He needed a mortal body, but there was vastly more to Jesus's mission than just the bit about bodies. We needed him. We were helplessly mortal, estranged, and confused. In response to our desperate need for reconciliation, Christ came to live life *with us* and *for us*. That shared identity with Christ was the story of Gethsemane. In that garden, he opened his heart fully to us in all our awfulness, walking with us through every possible terrible thing we've ever done or experienced. He let himself be racked body and soul by the terrible pain of loving mortals in all their pain and wretchedness. This communing love with us, such troubled and troubling mortals, is the story of Atonement. Christ's life was not fully his. It was ours as well.

If we allow ourselves to see the context of Christ's life, we realize that it wasn't the noun that Jesus called us to reject in his notorious sermons about losing lives. It wasn't "life" that Jesus asked us to hate. On the contrary, it was the possessive pronoun. Jesus asked us to despise the "his," the "my" that limits life to a single person. Life is to be loved and lived, and that is to be done together. Janette Hales Beckham, former Young Women General President and state legislator, made a similar point in more familiar terms: "The key to self-esteem is looking for the good in others."[5]

The Book of Mormon continues the witness of the New Testament, especially in the book of Mosiah. As King Benjamin was summarizing the meaning of his own life, preparing to turn the reins of the kingdom over to his son, Mosiah, he wanted people to know the meaning of their lives. His sermon is one of the great passages in the Book of Mormon. We should read it often and carefully. As part of a prolonged introduction, Benjamin emphasizes the focus of his royal ministry by indicating that he has "been suffered to spend [his] days in" the "service" of his people (Mosiah 2:12). He reminds his people, by way of exposing them to the shape of a life in Christ, that he has not tried to profit from their trust or his service. There was no tax for his support, no salary for him to draw, no special advantage he claimed.

King Benjamin seems to realize halfway through his renunciation of the advantages usually seized by kings that talking too much about his own service risks the paradoxical result of self-aggrandizement. In contemporary terminology, he may be worried about "humble bragging." So to avoid the sin of self-righteousness, Benjamin makes a crucial clarification; he acknowledges that his greatest allegiance is to other people and through those people to God: "I do not desire to boast, for I have only been in the service of God. And behold, I tell you these things that ye may learn wisdom; that ye may

---

5. Janette Hales Beckham, interview by Kate Holbrook, August 23, 2016, 14, Church History Library, Salt Lake City. I thank Kate Holbrook for this reference.

learn that when ye are in the service of your fellow beings ye are only in the service of your God" (Mosiah 2:16–17). It's a beautiful and powerful passage that many of us have committed to memory.

In the past, I've understood Benjamin's statement in the basic sense that we ought to perform more service. Charitable service is good, and God wants us to be of use to each other. I've often used Benjamin's discourse to motivate myself to do a better job as a Church member. I realize now as I return to this scripture as an adult that this is also a sermon about identity. Remember that the lead-up to this passage is Benjamin's characterization of the life of a king, the figure who might have the most reason for narcissism. Instead of finding himself in expressive individualism, though, Benjamin says that the meaning of his life, his identity as the king, is in service to other people and to God. He doesn't want to tell stories about his authentic self. He wants to tell stories about God and the people he serves, because they are who he is.

Scores of other scriptures tell similar stories brimming with important answers to that ever-familiar and vitally important question. *Who am I?* I am the people I love and who love me. *Who am I?* I am the God I love and who loves me. *Who am I?* I am a vessel of God's sanctifying grace. To the extent that I look inside myself, if I am fortunate, I glimpse that grace as it tumbles like rain from heaven to earth. This is the sacred dance we are called to live as Saints. It's the dance many of us have learned and lived from the very beginnings of the Restoration.

Jesus would celebrate with us aspects of our modern world, especially our aversion to cruelty. He wouldn't mind our love of the world as a vessel of his grace and the divine presence of our Heavenly Parents. Not at all. He lived under the stars in the stark and lovely hills and hollows of ancient Israel. For his parables he chose themes that touched on herding sheep, sowing seeds, and growing olives. In his gorgeous and sustaining Sermon on the Mount, he called us to remember God's tender and specific regard for the wildflowers and the swallows (see Matthew 6:25–30). Christ and his divine parents loved our world so much that they sent him to consecrate and restore it. On the other hand, he would be deeply uncomfortable with other aspects of our modern understanding. I think he would be alternately mystified and horrified to hear that sometimes we pretend to believe that the personhood that matters to eternity lives primarily inside individuals, apart from their relationships. Or that we can find the meaning and purpose of our mortal lives by looking in the mirror and expecting to see our own reflection. He would be baffled by categories and classes trumping membership in the body of Christ as the ways people make sense of each other.

Christ's stories about identity haunt me. I've had to try to learn his lessons many times. As often as not, I have failed. A paired success and failure from my mission may serve to illustrate the point. On my mission I was at my worst when I was concerned with my reputation as a committed and obedient proselytizer. I was at my best when I forgot myself in the sacred love of a broken soul hungry for the presence of God.

I worked hard to love a troubled family in New Orleans. We'll call the parents Ron and Deb. The gentle but tortured husband, Ron, was a lapsed Latter-day Saint. His drinking problem flared up while we were teaching Deb the discussions. He disappeared one night, and Deb called us in distress. Through tears she pleaded with us to find Ron. My companion and I headed out into Baton Rouge's hot, wet night following a combination of prayer and intuition. After forty minutes of searching, we felt to take the road to the right. Cresting a small hill, our headlights rested on Ron's form, asleep on a bus bench. We recognized him instantly. Ron's expression when he opened his eyes was that of a toddler on Christmas morning. "You are angels. You're here to save me," he told us in syllables that stumbled over each other. We took him to

52

our missionary apartment to sleep off his intoxication while we were at zone conference the next day. My companion and I didn't matter. Our love for Ron mattered. I got that right. Whatever happened next, we had carried God's love to one who suffered.

We do not control the world. Ron's drinking soon worsened, and the family fell further into poverty and pain. I began diverting my missionary stipend to cover their food and rent. I discovered that I could live on Winn-Dixie brand macaroni and cheese smothered in tabasco sauce for about fifty cents a day. That felt like a moral victory.

My companion and I moved deeper and deeper into the problems of Ron's and Deb's lives. We began to realize that they sometimes deceived us to try to manage chaos and maintain the sympathy they hoped would keep us loyal. And there began the failure, so soon after success.

Ron turned to me once, nervous, to tell me that Deb had been pregnant for over a year but there was no baby to show for it. We hadn't heard about a pregnancy before then. Ron seemed puzzled but afraid to be too curious lest it upset their relationship. Suspicious, I pushed to investigate. I think I started out believing that I wanted to be sure Deb was getting appropriate medical care, but my intentions were, as I later saw, grossly selfish. We came up with a hare-brained scheme to visit her medical clinic and get the truth. This was in the years before health privacy laws were much enforced, but what we did was indecent. We asked the nurse whether there was anything we, as the ministers at her church, should be doing to support Deb's late-stage pregnancy. We then listened in the waiting room as the weary clinic doctor blurted to his nurse, "What do you mean, she's pregnant?" Cruel detectives, we had solved the mystery and vindicated ourselves. We left the clinic and, shortly after, their lives.

Even now I don't know the best way to support families devastated by poverty, mental illness, and substance abuse.

Good-hearted, bright people disagree about the right modes of assistance and support; the risks of what some call "code-pendency" are real. But I do know that what I did to Deb was wrong. I'm ashamed even now to remember it. As best I can tell, my sin was the sin of narcissism. I needed to be right, to know whether she was lying. I didn't pause to plumb the depths of her wounds, or attempt to understand the pain, fear, and loneliness that underlay her pseudocyesis, a term I learned years later in medical school meant delusional pregnancy.

I'm not alone in this error. Many of us find that our service arises from mixed motivations. We aspire well but we often misunderstand the reasons why we do even the good things that we do. During a September 2018 devotional, Carolina Núñez, a dean at BYU's law school, shared a story of a visit to a community resource for LGBTQ teens. Although she entered with grand plans for the service she would provide, Dean Núñez recalls, "I was struck by the sense of community and closeness I felt there and by how quickly this new circle of friends had opened up to us. I left [the resource center] that day not as the rescuer I had imagined myself to be but as the rescued."[6] Realizing her own deep need, she understood the inescapable paradox of our identity—it arises in concert with others. Her story and confusions point gently to a major need we all have to repent, to see one another in both our specificity and our belonging.

In the middle of life, as I've stepped away from authenticity, I find myself fully committed to sincerity and genuineness.[7] The opposite of authenticity is not hypocrisy. In rejecting authenticity, I am drawing attention to the fact that our standards for genuineness represent an alignment with truth and beauty beyond us. When we are honest or sincere—when

---

6. Carolina Núñez, "Loving our Neighbors" (devotional address at Brigham Young University, September 18, 2018), https://speeches.byu.edu.

7. On the distinction, see Lionel Trilling, *Sincerity and Authenticity* (Cambridge: Harvard University Press, 1973).

we develop and manifest integrity—we are seeking to align our lives and our behaviors with something greater and better than we are. This is not a story about obliteration of our selves. As we are honest about who we are—a dazzling combination of individual choices and shared history and commitments to family and friends plus a combination of gifts, talents, and vulnerabilities—we will find ways to contribute to the gospel work as the vessels we genuinely are.

My skepticism about authenticity is thus not a call for sameness. We are instruments in an orchestra, and whatever instrument we are, we should play to the best of our ability. No orchestra benefits from a viola pretending to be an oboe or a flute substituting for a piano. But neither can an orchestra function if the bass demands that it be the only instrument or the trombone requires that it have a solo in every movement or if there are no violins at all. Problems of identity and community have always been a question of harmony and balance. Modern authenticity rhetoric bends our lives, both individual and community, out of balance. I believe that Jesus's call to move beyond authenticity will have unexpected implications in the world we now inhabit—this is not a question of conservatives or liberals, of traditionalists or antitraditionalists. The call to interdependent genuineness in the presence of Christ will stretch all of us across the political and social differences that would otherwise divide us.

The Church is the body of Christ and the fellowship of Saints. It is other people, knit together in their love of our Heavenly Parents. This knitting together is not a call for us to be stereotypically identical. The point in this kind of heavenly love is to belong in our differences, to consecrate ourselves and our *selves*. I want to pause at that word "consecrate." Many now may be tempted to think that consecration in this context means abandonment, the entire erasure of ourselves within the body of Christ. But to consecrate means to make holy as a gift to God, to see anew. As a consecrated Saint, I'm in many respects the same odd duck I've always been. To think that consecration means annihilation is to think like a modern secularist—that's a flat and limited view of what we are. What God asks of us is the unity in diversity of a body (see 1 Corinthians 12) whose members are as different from each other as eyes are from spleens and brains are from biceps. Here, always, we must be attentive to balance. God does not call us to perfect uniformity; nor does he call us to deep division. God calls us to a harmony of love and respect.

There's a paradox at the center of these questions, one that Christ clearly evoked in his teaching about the need to lose our lives to find them. We really can't know ourselves alone; authenticity is no simple path to self-understanding. I've lived these stories of identity in my own life for decades now. My selfish commitment to myself was the root of much pain for the people who love me, perhaps especially for my wife. In retrospect, it took years of marriage for me to forget myself well enough to see her clearly. And, crucially, it wasn't until I began to really know her that I had even a shot at knowing myself. I had to forget myself to know the meaning of life, including my own. I had to forget my modern ideas about myself and my authentic identity to find the world of love that hovered above me like God brooding over the waters of chaos in Genesis 1. As a husband and father, as a human being, I am continually called to forget myself: this is when my life really matters and the world comes alive with meaning and power. It's when I forget myself that I can see the Spirit of Christ filling the world with light and love. In that forgetfulness I find, as if by serendipity but really by grace, my soul enlarged.

So where does all this leave us in our own lives? These are theological but also fundamentally practical problems. We will remember King Benjamin's advice that we need not run faster than we have strength. We will try and fail and try and fail again. So will the people we work to love, to whom we pledge our faithfulness. But we must remember that the greatest beauty, power, goodness, and truth available to us as mortals will always involve sneaking out from under the thumb of our self-regard. We will be blind as long as we stare into mortal mirrors. In Christ, bathed in the love of our Heavenly Parents which we bring to the world in our hearts and hands, we encounter the sacred possibility that we will discover, in our forgetting, that we have known ourselves all along.

Leroy and Me

There's an experience I've recounted many times over the course of two decades. It's a touchstone in my first years as a God-believer. It is also, as I've come to believe, not true. And therein lies another story.

As I described earlier, I spent Sunday evenings my freshman year of college volunteering in a homeless shelter at the Congregational Church around the block from the Latter-day Saint meeting house in Cambridge, Massachusetts. Once, the night before a midterm examination in organic chemistry, Leroy, a consistent guest, arrived at the shelter visibly intoxicated. He was drunk, he explained, in earnestly slurred syllables, because he had been assaulted the night before. Drinking was his coping mechanism, he admitted, inspecting my knees with bleary eyes. He had explained similar intoxications to skeptical service workers before. I was not his first mark.

Leroy looked like Albert Einstein after a hunger fast. His sinews bulged and flexed within the skin around every joint. There was a laxity in his bones, too: when he stood as erect as he could, his silhouette was a crescent moon. Drunk, he rambled with occasional verbal spasms, but I had known Leroy for several months, and he was a quiet man. Hesitant and deferential, he was always gentle with me. Leroy hailed from Michigan but had lived in Boston for many years. I assumed the brutal Midwestern winters had prepared him for the Boston cold, but his childhood seemed like no real consolation at the time.

Unfortunately, I had to enforce shelter rules about intoxication. I could understand the argument that drunk guests didn't belong in the shelter. The church basement was chaotic enough when people were in control of their cognitive function. But I couldn't bear the thought of Leroy on the streets again that night, so sad, so fragile. Whatever the actual chances of another assault, he wept through half-pronounced words that if he slept outside that night he would die. His fear that he would not survive the night discomfited me.

On an impulse I identified as the guidance of the Spirit, I asked Leroy to stay with me that night in my dorm room. I had a pair of bright green two-piece pajamas, a gift for some now-forgotten milestone in my life. He showered and changed into those pajamas; I slept in shorts and a T-shirt. By the time our production had wrapped up it was after three a.m., about the time I had planned to awaken to finish studying for the chemistry midterm. Leroy snored, and my floor was hard and bare; I finally fell asleep around four a.m., wrapped in a spare blanket. He couldn't sleep past sunrise, a habit I suspect he had acquired in long years of homelessness. We both arose shortly after six a.m. I gave him some clothes, took him to breakfast, and saw him on his way. He carried his bowed frame in the lively, otherworldly manner of a fairy.

I arrived at my midterm later that morning, exhausted but jubilant. It was my official policy that I did no schoolwork on Sunday. I reserved the Sabbath for church duties and volunteering at the homeless shelter. I was a strict sabbatarian.

The combination of undergraduate procrastination, refusal to study on the Sabbath, and time tending to Leroy meant that I approached the exam almost entirely unprepared. The test was difficult but manageable, until I reached the crux question. That item involved understanding which bonds might break and what new configurations the bonds would contort themselves into after such a rupture. In retrospect, the problem required the ability to imagine, in three dimensions, that a bond could twist around the main body of a molecule and plug into the opposite side. As I confronted the problem, though, all I could see was my exhaustion. The seconds stretched into minutes as I inspected the page. The molecular structure was Chinese calligraphy to me. The Tinker Toy models we had all bought to help us visualize molecules—gray plastic sticks and rainbow-colored atomic balls—lay useless on the desk in front of me.

I prayed for divine assistance. What else was I to do? In the language of the hopeful foolishness of youth, I told God that I had done his work the night before and that it was time for him to help me. My prayer did not feel as blasphemous in my mind then as it does now to confess it. In any case, that was my prayerful petition.

As I opened my eyes to inspect the plastic model on my desk, I felt pure intelligence pour into me. I realized immediately where the bond had to move. I rendered the core insight onto the examination paper seconds later.

After dinner, I slept for twelve hours. On Wednesday I checked the exam results and discovered that I had achieved the high score on the midterm; I later learned that I was one of a tiny handful of students to solve that crux problem. The warm glow of that Monday morning's answered prayer stayed with me for weeks, maybe months.

At the time, the organic chemistry revelation confirmed my fledgling faith in God. My Heavenly Parents would be with me, I knew, as I served those in need. That was bedrock truth. I still treasure those memories: the image of Leroy in my clean green pajamas, eyes brimming with gratitude; that moment of clear seeing when the bond between two atoms broke and a new one formed; the flood of gratitude I felt to God for allowing me to care for Leroy and still earn top marks on a difficult chemistry exam. For me, those tender memories and that glorious presence exemplify all that is best in a world filled with God.

It turns out, though, that this story isn't true.

I told it for a decade and a half. It felt true to me every time. I have clear memories of both Leroy in my dorm room and of the flash of inspiration that moved the bond around the outside of the molecule. There was no doubt in my mind that the story was true, an emblem of the abiding of God's grace with me in that first year of my life as a theist.

Then, in 2013, my mother decided that a forty-something could store his own darn memorabilia, which had sulked, untouched, in her garage for years. The souvenir boxes contained miscellaneous treasures dating as far back as my childhood in Helena, Montana and as far forward as medical school in Boston. Among them was a blue examination book from a course my freshman year of college, "The Bible and Its Interpreters." James Kugel, an Orthodox Jew who made a storied career of studying ancient Bible interpretation, taught a survey course that was one of the most popular undergraduate courses in the Harvard catalog. I signed up for the course because I was newly religious and curious about the Bible. I did not know that it was a notorious "gut." (No one could ever explain to me the etymology of the term, but it meant a course that gave high grades for minimal effort. Guts were popular among the athletes and aristocrats of fair Harvard.) On the cover of that blue book, I had written "Leroy" next to my A grade. The handwriting was clearly mine. I had personally dedicated the exam grade to my homeless bunkmate.

I felt the heat of embarrassment behind my eyes as I realized that this was the Monday midterm that had been divinely protected from fatigue—the one from my cherished story.

My first impulse was that the old me was wrong and the new me was right. Maybe I had written a note about Leroy years after the fact. I put my historian's hat on, though, and tested the account more rigorously. I realized that the old story was strictly impossible. I took organic chemistry my sophomore year because inorganic chemistry was a freshman-year prerequisite. But I volunteered at the First Church shelter my freshman year. And the Kugel course was definitely my freshman year.

With those facts in mind, I spent more time pondering, and slowly I remembered that after my mission, I was again fastidious about not doing any schoolwork on Sundays. I filled my life with church duties and general service (I tried to return to the shelter, but the rhythms had changed while I was away, and I couldn't find my place there anymore). I sometimes felt at a disadvantage because my peers used Sundays to study for Monday exams, and I did not. With more focused memory, I managed to recall that when I prayed during my organic chemistry exam, I was invoking the pedestrian sacrifices of Sabbath observance and church service. My dramatic slumber party with Leroy was in the distant past.

In retrospect, there were two distinct inputs—loving Leroy and refusing to study on Sunday—and two separate outputs—a high grade on an easy Bible midterm, and top marks on the organic chemistry exam. I had collapsed two events into one, storing them in my memory as the most satisfying input and the most compelling output. As for the input, I've been a Social Gospel Latter-day Saint for the entire course of my believing, so my tender care of Leroy was more satisfying in memory than being a rigid sabbatarian. On the output side, I don't think anyone would be surprised that I could score high marks in a notoriously easy course on the Bible. I was a readerly boy raised in and around the Church of Jesus Christ of Latter-day Saints, and I was good at taking tests. There was nothing especially miraculous about an A on Kugel's Bible midterm.

On this interpretation, my panic at not having studied for the Bible midterm was a manifestation of my competitive nature, even in an easy class. Organic chemistry is a different story. That's a subject that everyone knows will be difficult, and it's exciting to solve a problem, however simplified for undergraduates, of molecular structure. The compelling input and output had come together like peanut butter and jelly on two slices of bread.

But now the cats and the horses are out of their bags and barns. Loving Leroy did *not* solve a chemistry problem for me. My history had changed.

It took a while to reshape my memory to match the events I had reconstructed. I remember the experiences separately now, as distinct windows on my growing relationship with God and my navigation of the competing demands of religious and secular life. Because I am a fastidious academic and because I believe that we should embrace truth when we encounter it, I now recount the past as accurately as I can. Loving Leroy won me an A on an easy Bible midterm. Which was never really the point after all.

As I've considered this accident of history telling, I don't regret the story as I told it in the past. All along, the parable of Leroy and the midterm has been about sacrificing worldly success to make space for God and deep love in my life. There has always been in the story, too, the accidentally haughty boy who believes that God is bound to honor his righteous aspirations. Both of those elements—the joy of life in the presence of God and the undercurrent of arrogance that expects God to deliver blessings on command or to see acts of charity as money in a spiritual bank account—are present in the story as I once remembered it and as I now remember it. What is most important about the story survived the garage-cleaning revelations of 2013.

This experience with remembering Leroy and the mid-term has made me more sympathetic to those who have told their histories variably in the past. Who knows why my story changed? For the life of me, I have no memory of any conscious decision to tell the Leroy story the way I did, no moment when I wanted to look more the hero, no calculation of the ramifications of a particular narrative choice. I never sat down and said to myself, "How do I make myself look good?" It was an imperceptible movement through memory.

I see the old-now-new-again problem of our sacred history as Latter-day Saints with fresh eyes. Some of the stories we told in the past no longer seem quite true in their details, at least not in the way we thought. Leroy wasn't really the patron saint of organic chemistry undergraduates. The First Vision in the Pearl of Great Price is not the report of a field biologist studying divine visitations.

The First Vision is another story with a story, like Leroy and the chemistry exam, but far vaster. Starting with his embarrassment after a tongue lashing by a preacher he admired, Joseph Smith emphasized different aspects of the vision at different times—sometimes he emphasized the relevance of his own salvation, sometimes he emphasized that his and others' salvation depended on a functioning church restored to a special priesthood.[1] We Latter-day Saints have sometimes told this story as if it were in fact a science experiment, some moment when God was caught on camera. Much like me demanding that God finish my chemistry midterm for me, we as a church body have sometimes required that the First Vision solve our theological problems, simply and linearly. But the chemistry exam was never really about the exam. It was about the possibility that God cares about me, in all my twists and turns, in all my youthful arrogance. And the

1. See Steven Harper, *First Vision: Memory and Mormon Origins* (New York: Oxford University Press, 2019).

First Vision, as useful as it has been for honing our thinking and preaching, and as much as I do believe God visited the teenaged Joseph Smith, isn't really about proving some specific item of doctrine. It's about God caring about this boy and his family and those who would hear God's voice in that boy's sermons and scriptures. We've had our twists and turns in the telling of our sacred stories. And so did Joseph and his scribes. That's the living process of memory. That's part of mortal life in proximity to God.

Other aspects of our shared sacred history are similar to the First Vision. A dozen or so familiar stories about the first decades of the Restoration look different when viewed by professional historians than by contemporary Latter-day Saints. Sometimes readers are tempted to see these differences as marks of a nefarious plot of misinformation or intentional betrayal of trust. Often these differences have been flagged as "problems" with Church history. But I think we can be forgiven for imagining that the garbled nuances or the painful incongruities were never the main point in those stories. What mattered most shone through these traditions even in their mistransmission. And we have the capacity as we revisit those stories to continue to see clearly the real meanings that have been there all along.

I'm a scholar and a believer: pleasure in details is part of my makeup and always has been. Alongside the pleasure in getting minute details right stands a recognition of the humanity I share with those who have also tried to get their stories right—to tell the deep truth about the experiences they've had and remembered alongside the details. This work has connected them and me to the broader stories we humans tell about the nature of the world and its past. Misremembering and re-remembering are as much a part of us as the experiences we attempt to capture in memory. As I look back at Leroy and the undergraduate me, I'm struck more than anything by gratitude for the ability to participate in this life and to continue to try to make sense of it. I feel a similar invigoration when it comes to our shared history as Saints, remembering, misremembering, and remembering again as we make our way through life and history, in the quiet, faithful company of God.

PART TWO:
THE FEAST OF
THE SENSES

The Bread of Life, with Chocolate Chips

I learned to cook when my wife was recovering from cancer surgery. There's a hollowness, kindred to cancer, hungry to swallow you up when a beloved's life is threatened. I still remember, with a soul-deep ache, that time when her body was a battleground for monstrously mutated cells and scalpelling surgeons. Those harrowing days and our sudden awareness of her mortality still haunt me. I've seen a lot of death in my life; nothing disoriented me like her cancer.

The wild upheaval of unexpected illness unearthed more than a surgical specimen for the pathologist's microscope. She and I discovered in the cancer's aftermath my longstanding failure as a husband to be her full partner. This dereliction had insinuated itself into the infrastructure of our marriage. I realized that my soul needed a surgery of its own. The simultaneous, stark revelation of her mortality and my personal failure left me wanting to sit alone in a room and cry my way through the smothering chaos rather than accept the transformation that beckoned.

But there was no time to stare, heartbroken, at my pitiful soul, dithering about whether I could be remade, whether we could be made whole. I would have to man up. I would need to keep house. I would have to find a sacramental life, one more sacred and more ordinary than I had previously known.

The war between the forces of order and chaos is as ancient as any humanity we would recognize as our own. In the Bible's opening lines, our Hebrew God tamed the waters of the primordial abyss. The Hebrews' neighbors and occasional captors, the Babylonians, despised the waters of chaos too. In Babylon, the people celebrated the power of the god Marduk's sword to vanquish the sea monster Tiamat, who presided over the inundating waters. The Babylonians believed that the god-king's slaughter of that watery demon made human existence possible.

Those Babylonians are my kin. I know that chaos and detest it. I struggle against its asphyxiating wetness. In the weeks of our physical and psychic suffering, as I felt the waters of despair swell, I wanted to gut Tiamat to put an end to the chaos. I needed Marduk's sword but did not know where to find it. In its place, I grabbed a thick-bellied, well-balanced kitchen knife. It hefted well. I started chopping vegetables.

When she and I first met the summer after college, my kitchen consisted of an electric vegetable steamer made of thin plastic. In it I melted bags of Lipton pasta mixes into nodular slurries. Most nights, I half expected a two-headed brook trout with five eyes to peer up from the yellowish, lumpy mass. But I didn't care. Especially when mixed with a can of cold black beans, the molten pasta sustained me. I had other priorities than food.

She changed all that.

One of my first memories of our years together is of an outlet store hawking adventure clothing in southeastern Maine. On a whim, a friend who was with us rescued a bag of cookies abandoned by a forgetful shopper on top of a clothes rack. Still troubled by urban legends about razor blades concealed in Halloween apples, I refused to share in the spoils.

Surely, I fretted, a sociopath had baked the cookies with fox-glove before depositing them as bait above the fleece sweaters. But my wife, eyes singing with pleasure, partook. No razor blades, no poison herbs. Just butter, sugar, flour, and chocolate. She laughed at me, her mouth full of cookie. In the car afterward, I ran my fingers through her thick, black hair. I still feel that hair in the web spaces of my fingers, where it caught each time before I wiggled my hand free. For an hour as we drove up the Maine coast, my hand held that emblem of her mortality—the supple, sable threads of keratin that will persist for many years, maybe even centuries, after the two of us are gone. For those moments, I am pushing at the veil between life and death as she rests her head on my lap and I weave my fingers into her hair.

During the initial crisis, I cooked simple, even clumsy dishes. I flailed in a quicksand of risottos, week after week, gruels of sodden rice drowning in liquefied cheese. With time, though, she taught me the language of the kitchen. As she initiated me into the fellowship of the hearth, I opened my heart to the ancient rhythm of the village. I found myself drawn into the cycles that once organized the world. I saw harvest seasons as more than a Whole Foods marketing campaign. I considered what it might mean to handle a bundle of life moving into death—roasted carrots or a seared tenderloin, perhaps—on our hearth. I felt connected, however tenuously, to the ancient patterns of temple sacrifice, the rituals that continue to echo in the bread and water of the sacrament. I began to see that where there is partaking, there is also giving.

Once she had recovered from her surgeries, my wife guided my culinary restlessness into intermittently successful experiments. I learned how to attend to the moment when the cumin, coriander, and garlic splash into sweetly diaphanous onions bathing in hot oil. That tiny explosion of odors still recalls to my increasingly sentimental memory those early years as her pupil.

She did not, however, teach me to bake. I was afraid. The distracted nonchalance of stove work fit my personality. I could stab some specimen of Allium or whittle a fennel bulb, smear the sacrifice in oil and salt, and start it on fire. Vivid flavor could spring from death, no matter the liberties I took with the instructions. I could add extra salt, or vinegar, or Aleppo chili pepper flakes at the end, as our tongues dictated. Baking, on the other hand, channeled the stern wisdom of endless generations of ancestors whose culinary science was hard-won and ironclad. Baking meant gardening in fastidious colonies of yeast. It demanded precision. In baking, the ways I touched and handled wet, leavened flour created the difference between pleasure and distress. The baker's tasks entailed reading recipes as if they were binding law. I preferred to see recipes as half-remembered oral traditions eager to evolve.

I observed her, though, enthralled by her careful face and the tawny blubber of dough that she massaged with her hands before lowering it into a bread pan. I watched her create cakes from cocoa, butter, and flour. Baking was perilous, yes, but also beautiful. Before we could partake, we would need to create.

In the misery after her first surgery, a box of fine chocolates arrived on our doorstep from San Francisco. They were a gift from a friend, a whimsical, quantitative man whose mind never sleeps. The exquisite flavors of that chocolate told us a story about the meaning of life. We will all die, and most of us will suffer. And yet we will have known the tenderly bitter tang of chocolate shared with a beloved, the sweet softness of homemade bread in a quiet kitchen, the touch of fingertips and oil on our scalps during healing blessings. We will have given and partaken. We will have lived.

After a few years of cooking, I happened upon Kristine Wright's essay about Latter-day Saint women baking bread for the sacrament. Not allowed to perform the formal priesthood ordinance, they brought the ritual to life in the loaves of bread

74

they offered on the altar.[1] They baked the Lord's presence into the world, recapitulating his work in Capernaum. There, Jesus had performed his great miracle of loaves and fishes. Five thousand men, plus (we suspect) an equal number of women and children, listened to Jesus with one ear and their grumbling stomachs with the other. He fed them from a basket of food barely adequate to sate the hunger of his disciples, let alone the multitude. The crowd would be hungry again within a few hours, but for those moments, the barley loaves and dried fish were sufficient to teach them that Jesus was the Bread of Life. In his eternal presence, his divinity mapped onto human transience, he is our everlasting bread. He is the force that makes us whole in spirit and body. The sacrament bread is our access to his broken body, yes, but it is also our access to the sacred give and take of mortality. We bake, and we eat. We give, and we partake. The sacrament is an ancient story not only about Calvary and the Passover meal just before it. The sacrament is also about the wedding at Cana, the miracles at Capernaum, and the morsels of flatbread Jesus shared with his followers as they walked the dusty paths of life.

The thought of baking sacramental bread as a ritual in its own right captivated me. If Jesus was the Bread of Life, those Latter-day Saint women were his bakers. I realized then that women had also likely baked the bread of that Passover meal transformed by Jesus's broken body. When he gave thanks at that last supper, it was for their bread. I knew in my soul's soul that when Jesus preached the Bread of Life, he had in mind those women baking that bread. I could taste their bread in the same place of knowing. I could hear believers praying, as Jesus taught them, for *that* daily bread whenever they turned their eyes to the sky. There is in the sacrament not only the

---

1.   Kristine Wright, "'We Baked a Lot of Bread': Reconceptualizing Mormon Women and Ritual Objects," in *Women and Mormonism: Historical and Contemporary Perspectives*, ed. Kate Holbrook and Matthew Bowman (Salt Lake City: University of Utah Press, 2016), 82–100.

twelve disciples at the Last Supper. There is also Mary and Martha and the scores of nameless women who shared the bread of their hearths with this mysterious man who would one day die on a cross and another day rise from the dead in defiance of all the sadness and cruelty in the world.

In the bread of the Lord's Supper, eternity and time come together. That crushed wheat mixes with water and yeast, is lit on fire, and enters our bodies, where we burn it again in our cellular furnaces. There is fire everywhere. The baking fires remind me of the scriptural accounts of baptism by fire. In the scriptures this fire refers to the Holy Ghost (see Matthew 3:11; Doctrine and Covenants 19:31) or the refiner's purifying fire (see Malachi 3:2; 3 Nephi 24:2; Doctrine and Covenants 128:24). I tend to see that phrase in those twin senses of spirit and transformation. When my own baptism by fire will come, I do not know. I suspect it began with those cancer surgeries and the wounds they exposed. But we all dance in that refining fire on the boundary between eternity and time whenever we bake. Christ's gift has always been in his grace-filled juxtaposition of the eternal and the temporary. He brings that merger into our inward parts and etches it there. I am not surprised now that we would enter Christ's life each week as we prayerfully eat a thumb-sized piece of bread and a swallow of water, emblems gone by the time we have realized we are eating them.

As I reflected on those sisters baking that sacramental bread, I remembered the chocolates that arrived in the midst of our cancered sadness. Those two images—of baking bread and delivering chocolates—braided themselves together as I entered a new phase of my religious life. In new circumstances, I discovered a way to bring the mystery, power, and ordinariness of the sacrament into the patterns of ministry to those I come into contact with.

Years into my apprenticeship in the kitchen, some well-intentioned church leaders decided that I should serve as an elders quorum president. I couldn't imagine why anyone thought I belonged in a hierarchy. My persona is on my best days disheveled, and my belief, however fervent, is often clumsy. I doubted that I could be of any use as a leader on behalf of the people we worshiped with. I'm sincere but socially awkward, and I am terrible at small talk. My attempts to love and support other people often don't make sense to them. I saw that I needed a way to communicate affection and respect in a language that the recipients of that affection would understand.

This felt like no small feat. I realized, in the rare clarity of thought I associate with inspiration, that I'd better learn to bake. To my mind, a ministry intended to recall Jesus's would need to again incarnate his bread of life, even if the leaven was chemical, and sugar and chocolate joined hands with the flour. Cookies were small and lively; they were more manageable than bread, more easily shared with ward members. Plus, chocolate chip cookies are the first and most familiar of sweet baked things, a common pathway into the guild of those who know flour and water. An ever-gracious mentor, my wife taught me a basic recipe for salted chocolate chip cookies based on whole-wheat flour. I was a mediocre student of baking, as I had feared. But her attention and my belief that God wanted me to bake called me to persevere. Gradually, vivid flavors started coming through, especially when I began zesting citrus peels into the dough. The veil of fear and unfamiliarity over my eyes began to lift.

The veil. It's a story about being blind and yet feeling the warm breath of another, greater realm on our cheeks. This veil of mortality drapes across the world to separate the living from the dead. On our mortal side of this supernatural curtain stand the people whose stomachs rumble, who yawn and sweat and fight and want. On the other side of that boundary, it's all of us a century later, now pure and godly. As a young child, I imagined the veil as if it were cheesecloth wrapped around a quorum of ghosts. I still like that image of a gauzy barrier at which the living and dead strain to see and be seen. I'm glad to love and be loved by those who have slipped from the world-that-can-be-touched into the world beyond our fingertips. The more time I've spent in the kitchen, the more persuaded I am that the sacrament as a ritual permeates our lives and makes the veil occasionally lighter.

Increasingly, I think of the veil as the barely visible interface between what is temporary and specific on the one hand and what is eternal and universal on the other. It's that shimmer just out of sight when we look over an alpine lake at dusk. It is, in the company of the beloved, the shiver of awareness that my wife is not just an electrified scaffold of gristle and bone. The veil contains the sacred yearning that comes as we eat the bread of life. The veil is the promise of life in the midst of physical and spiritual deaths. The veil wraps tight around us as we "take, eat" the blessed bread and its wine-as-water.

When she and I stand together in the kitchen, the veil of eternity stretches under the pressure of our kneading fingers. As the remnants of plants and animals speed their dissolution over the fire of our modern stove, they place us in a different kind of time. These living things-becoming-food, these cookies and loaves of already broken bread, are real. So are we, both broken and real, in time and eternity. These baked things, along with the bakers themselves, are the earthy emblems of Jesus's broken body.

We Christians eat in remembrance of a God beaten to death. We do it every Sunday as we take the sacrament. The Lord's Supper isn't just about that one Passover meal, though, however carefully we repeat it. We are always eating, our lives as fragile as food. From the sacrifices of animal and vegetable spring our enfleshed souls. When we make ourselves vulnerable to the flavors born of these foods and the communities they may cohere, we push our fingers into the veil.[2] Our spirits surge with a life greater than our bodies can contain.

I get, I think, what the ancients were doing with their animal sacrifices, so much more daring and wildly natural than our searing the flesh of dismembered factory chickens over machined rows of propane flames. Our ancestors slaughtered, gutted, and divided a sheep into a wood fire to burn it into fragrant smoke that would feed the heavens an eternal meal. We need, as they needed, to melt the veil of eternity into our lives. Our Hebrew predecessors did so at the temple altar; we do it at the sacrament table. I troubled that veil in my ministry with chocolate chip cookies.

These cookies my wife taught me to bake have become a spiritual discipline for me, like a nun worrying the beads of her rosary. I bake them almost every week now. Because my grandfather loved puns, I dubbed them the "cookies of the priesthood," as they were intended to entice the elders to visit our Spartan classroom above the staircase. But this clownish pun about sacred keys hid the truth. I was dead earnest. I couldn't stop thinking about the sacramental bread when I baked them. That bread was the otherworldly priesthood of the firstborn made actual among us. My cookies were a vastly humbler offering than the sacrament emblems. They were Jesus as the Bread of Life and the bread he broke with the disciples. They were the sacrificial offering Abraham and Sarah made to Melchizedek. They were the Savior hanging from a cross and calling out for his father absent in heaven as his mother wept at his feet. They are the soul-healing promise of his broken body. They are the assurance that in opening ourselves to eternity we can see through the death of spirit and body, that Atonement is concerned with more than just a blessedly quiet afterlife wrapped in the veil's ghostly gauze. I do not mean that these cookies

---

2. Steven Peck, "Death and the Ecological Crisis," *Agriculture and Human Values* 27, no. 1 (2010): 105–9 has influenced my thinking on our dependence on the death of both animal and vegetable life.

replace the formal ordinances that structure our Church life. Not at all. But as I watch the extension of the divine presence brought to earth in ordinances, I see that holy presence shimmering in the baking I do for the people I love and whom I hope to love.

Sometimes these cookies, much as the sacramental meal they extend in space and time, are a hope of solace in the face of personal tragedy, like when a friend's father died unexpectedly. Sudden death hideously breaks the living and the dead. Survivors must bear that rupture in their souls. My friend's favorite cookies were pumpkin chocolate chip, so we baked fifty small, orange-brown cakes studded with chocolate chips and left them on their back porch with a note of condolence. I realized as I walked back up the street that these priesthood cookies were my offering against death.[3] I had little else. In such despair, sometimes we can only say "take, eat," as we hold hands in otherwise silent support. Those chocolates, that sadness, are the bread of life in the mouths of mortals. We are broken as the bread is broken; we are remade in that life-giving bread.

That calamitous death taught me that many events that call us to protest our infirmity also welcome a morsel of this bread of life. Funerals, cancers, heart attacks, drug overdoses, and advancing birthdays after middle age all want the cookies of that priesthood of Christ, the priesthood that thins the veil between our fingers. This bread of life, bedecked with chocolate chips, is my testimony of hope against cataclysm.

We're going to die one day, she and I. So will everyone we have ever known and loved. That day will come long before we desire it. And yet, in the meanwhile, we will bake, we will break bread, we will give, and we will wonder as the veil wraps close about our skin.

---

3. I use "priesthood" here in the broader sense, associated with temple and family, that flows through both men and women in hopes of drawing attention to the ways that this priesthood is at home in the kitchen as well as the temple.

Redemption and the
Work of Opera

My first experience with opera did not go well. My wife and I joined our oldest daughter's godparents at the Metropolitan Opera, America's greatest stage for this exuberant and pretentious art form. I was bored and mystified. From my perspective, barely visible figures shouted at each other at the bottom of an open pit mine. We were perched at the mine's upper rim, trying to decipher the red supertitles that flickered on the backs of most seats. I insisted that we leave at the intermission, disappointing my wife's hope that her boorish husband could appreciate high culture. In preparation, she'd taught me to love the movie *Moonstruck*, which treated *La Bohème* as an object of otherworldly beauty. The Met in person couldn't compete in my imagination with Cher and Nicolas Cage.

When my wife lost her eye to cancer a decade later, I yearned, heartsick, to live thoughtfully and in the presence of beauty beyond the everyday. If mortal life will be so fleeting, so uncertain, so painful, then at least I would celebrate what is beautiful. I'd always loved choral music and have generally preferred hymns to sermons. I wondered whether I'd done right by opera with that first indifferent encounter with the Met. I'd seen posters at local movie theaters advertising high-definition opera broadcasts. I decided to give it a try, just once, on the off chance that opera was, in fact, beautiful.

I was spellbound. Wowed into silence, I could only watch and listen as Pushkin's old poem, *Eugene Onegin*, came to life. That proud, dumb man and the glorious woman who grew beyond his scorn told their stories in melodies and harmonies mapped out by Tchaikovsky. I loved it all. The voices. The effulgent, thrumming harmonies of strings and singers. The visual imagery. The costumes. The stage. The gentle, haunting exoticism of sung Russian. I even, I confess, loved the smell of the popcorn in my lap.

I realized that day that opera is a total art form. The many levels of its art pushed me toward sensory overload. I felt I had made contact, however imperfect, with the glories of another world through the combination of singing, orchestral music, costumes, stage, and story. I imagined to myself that, in this spectacle, I witnessed a foreshadowing of the vast community that constitutes heaven, a network of radically distinct individuals united into consummating harmony.

However sublime opera is as an art form, though, the plots themselves are laughable. Half of them are as dimwitted as boys snickering in a locker room. They're mostly quick sketches of sex, violence, betrayal, and mistaken identity. The few plots that take the time and energy to really aspire to anything memorable generally end up convoluted and overwrought. Richard Wagner is notorious for such unwieldy plots, which groan under the metaphysical weight he piles on top of them. A friend of mine, an accomplished soprano herself, complains to me that she hates how stupid, thin, and scandalous the opera stories are. She's right about that fact, but for me the beauty is in the soulful work of opera rather than the integrity of the plots.

This juxtaposition of the brilliant and the banal stands at the center of our current lives. This is the miracle of Incarnation. This is the fact that we are silly, aching, trivial mortals staggering under the gravity of our divine essence. The only really smart thing I think I've ever heard attributed to Sigmund Freud (and even then he was just riffing on biblical teaching) is when he called human beings the gods who poop (he used a more graphic word for our waste). This is the staggering reality—we are marvelous, conscious, and yearning for the divine, and yet we void waste from our bowels and bladders, say awful things, betray each other, and succumb to injury, cancer, and deformity. We are all of those things that belong to heaven or to earth. So is opera.

Take the beloved aria "Nessun dorma," from Puccini's *Turandot*. The opera is a weird, even cheesy, epic about a princess who plays exceptionally hard to get. She sets mostly impossible tasks for her suitors to accomplish. One persistent prince manages to complete the tasks, but she still resists marrying him. He agrees that if she can discover his name before sunrise he will liberate her from the obligation of marriage. The prince, confident that even though she has called for the entire kingdom to stay awake all night to discover his name, mocks her by singing "nessun dorma," *no one shall sleep*. It's a nonsensical moment in a silly story. But the song is so majestic that Luciano Pavarotti turned it into a blockbuster. He sang it at football games to the rousing cheers of many thousands of inebriated sports fans. The song is spectacular. When I hear it—almost every time—I want to clap, laugh, and cry all at once. But it's basically a few lines from a Disney princess movie, sung perfectly. Such is the juxtaposition of the beautiful and silly in opera. Such is the work of our lives.

We as believers shouldn't be surprised by this. We adore a Savior who condescends to be in our midst, who held together in his mortal person the mysteries of the human and divine realms. Ours is a Savior born to the poverty of a displaced family and stored in a makeshift barn, sleeping in a grimy feed trough, spackled in the spittle of sheep and rotted food. He was a divine Savior born as an infant who bawled and soiled himself and had to learn to walk and speak.

I once attended an intimate discussion group with several prominent Christian professors. They asked what I did to try to place myself into a spiritual attitude that could make me available to inspiration from God. I told them that I listened to opera. They agreed that, sure it's nice to encounter beautiful art sometimes, smiling at me as if I were a benign and uncomprehending student. But they didn't understand my spiritual life, and they didn't understand opera. This marvelous merger of beauty and banality is for me a pathway to the spirit and presence of God. Making myself open to the reality of the sublime and the preposterous unfolds to me the secrets of life, afterlife, and their interconnected meanings. Such is the work of opera on my life, the work of God in my soul.

In the silly and the sublime often stands the work of redemption. Sometimes we are brought up short by something perfectly, undeniably true, however modest its clothing. I have witnessed that promise of redeeming love in an opera by an old German composer whose music drives my wife crazy. She dry-heaves when I even mention his name. I guess I don't blame her. If you're not in the mood, his music can sound like a retired glamour metal band strumming power chords with their fists. It's adolescent and silly. But Wagner's music is much more than that to me.

I first encountered Wagner, as I suspect did many of my generation, through the brutal surf scene on the beach in the Vietnam war film *Apocalypse Now*. "The Ride of the Valkyries" is dizzy, wild, frightening stuff. I was hooked the moment I heard it blaring from the speakers installed on the outrigger of the army helicopter. It helps that Wagner's a bit medievalesque in his musical sensibilities, as if J. R. R. Tolkien's Elven stories had been arranged for orchestra and singers. There's something downright pleasurable in Wagner's campy enthusiasm. I'm aware of all his social and political troubles. I'm not naïve. I hate that he was a German nationalist and that his art was later put to malignant purposes by Nazis. Those aspects of his life and legacy nauseate me.

Wagner's awful character flaws notwithstanding, several of his operas have been vessels of divine wisdom to me, *Tannhauser* most of all.

As I've said, the silly plots of opera are the latticework for a stunning union of music and passion. In *Tannhauser*, the protagonist is a musician who has been seduced by the goddess Venus to live with her in a purely sensual world. Tannhauser breaks free of Venus's grasp and returns to Germany, where the lovely and virtuous Elisabeth has been awaiting his return. He tries to reintegrate into human society but immediately violates Elisabeth's trust and publicly humiliates her. He can't help himself. Elisabeth's friends and peers turn against him in anger, swords drawn. They even appear to be calling for his execution. It's an absurd tableau.

But Elisabeth changes all that. She, the wronged person, throws herself between drawn swords and her awful boyfriend. She says, in essence, that Tannhauser is not beyond redemption. Whatever her friends' rage tells them, this fallen musician can still be redeemed. Elisabeth thus spares his life. Tannhauser disappears into pilgrimage, where he learns that he is as likely to be made whole as a wooden staff is to bloom like a live tree branch. He is lost.

Elisabeth dies, grieving Tannhauser's fate. Tannhauser finally disavows Venus and dies of holy grief on discovering Elisabeth's death, just as we hear the Pilgrim's Chorus return to us the exciting and promising melody of the overture that began our journey with this strange and sensual musician. The pilgrims have come to announce that the pope's staff has in fact sprouted a leaf as if it were still alive. Two impossible events have occurred: Tannhauser has been redeemed, and dead wood has come to life.

There's a lot to process in *Tannhauser*. The plot is thin and idiosyncratic. It's about as goofy as opera usually is. The kinky ballet at the beginning is distracting at best. The music is beautiful. The story is sad. And there's a fulcrum in the opera that continues to bind me.

My mind keeps returning to the moment when Elisabeth throws herself between Tannhauser and the angry crowd clamoring for his death. I remember the woman brought to Jesus for judgment in John 8. She'd been found having sex with a man she wasn't married to, or so the crowd reported. They hoped that Jesus the Jewish holy man would sanction their decision to stone her. In a cryptic way that has stymied centuries of interpreters, Jesus told the mob that this woman was not beyond redemption. Whatever law she might have violated, she could be made whole. The community could not expel her. He would not be complicit in her death.

In some sense, that is the entire story of Christ's ministry: it is to discover the possibility that we broken human beings can be made whole. None of us is beyond God's powerful love. Not even the worst of us.

Where I work in the intensive care unit, complex machines can maintain life despite every biological indication that death has come. Often, although not always, we win this strenuous contest with the specter of death. That is the exciting, dramatic side of the world of the ICU, the part often portrayed on television. But this story forgets, as so often happens, the spiritual side of our work. In the ICU we are striving to be true to Elisabeth's example. The patients who need my services are often a *Who's Who* of the people Christ loves when no one else seems to. Drug addicts and alcoholics, homeless men and women, people with terrible psychiatric illnesses, people with advanced illness or other signs of oppressive physical weakness. Some of them have intentionally done themselves harm and are struggling to imagine that their lives could have any worth. They are the weak who, some say—with increasing fervor in recent years—would be better off dead anyway.

As I returned to work after encountering *Tannhauser*, I realized more clearly than ever that I'm not just called to operate life support systems with technical precision. I'm called to protest that these weak and unloved people still stand within the scope of redemption. I must sing with Elisabeth, who sings with Christ, that I will be a witness to their hidden dignity. I will see the light that shimmers in and through them, whatever their physical limitations.

In my personal life, too, I am called to realize that if I want to be like Jesus, I will need to sing Elisabeth's song. Tannhauser is not beyond redemption; the worst and most frustrating people I know are within the scope of love and respect. No one is beyond redemption, not even Wagner.

I'm still not as good at this calling as Elisabeth was. I'm liable by nature to avert my eyes, to walk away, to refuse to see many of the people who cross my path. But I am trying. When I stop, prayerfully, I hear her song, I see her face. And I work a little harder. In that work I see through these mortal farces and limitations to what is lovely and eternally true. I see the truth in life and in opera: together, the sublime and the absurdly human are all I could ever want.

The Scent
of the Gospel

I went to dinner one evening with some of my wife's colleagues, professional scholars of religion. One, a thoughtful and well-regarded student of American Catholicism, asked about the scent he had detected during a temple open house on his visit to the Wasatch Front. He thought it might have been incense and wondered whether, as with the Catholic Mass, there was a place for sacred smoke in Mormon temple worship. I don't blame him. Even if it's not my religious tradition, I like the smell of a Catholic Mass. We reassured him that Latter-day Saints don't use incense in their sacred rituals, and the conversation rapidly transitioned to a practical sort of question: what *is* the typical scent of our church?

To me, other than the bright savor of infants babbling, cooing, or shouting their way through sacrament meeting, there is one smell more than any other that brings the Church to my mind: olive oil pressed onto a warm scalp.

That smell, in a vivid nutshell, is the story of the restored gospel in my soul.

Olive oil is an ancient companion for humans. For thousands of years our ancestors have used this balm of the fruit of the *Olea europaea* tree for cooking, for smoothing cracked skin, for signaling what matters, even for anointing their rulers. And, in millennia of traditions that extend well beyond the Christian Bible, they have used olive oil for healing.

We have only rare verses in the New Testament to tell us that the Christian elders anointed sufferers with oil in their time of need (see Mark 6:13; James 5:14). We know from other sources that throughout the ancient Mediterranean, oil was a sacred emollient used for many anointings, both secular and religious. These ancient practitioners inhabited a world vastly different from ours. They had no pump bottles of skin lotion, no real pharmaceuticals, and at best only rudimentary surgery. But they also lived in a world charged with meanings and powers that many of us have lost, as we have abandoned our childhood wonder and our knowledge of the way grass feels against bare feet and extended palms.

My first personal encounter with olive oil was during flu season in the late 1970s. I've never had influenza before or since, thank heavens, but I still remember the sense of being squeezed in a hot vise as the Hong Kong virus poured through my bloodstream. My body ached in terrible heat. I lay rigid in the center of the living room floor, my father and a pair of home teachers standing over my still-warm corpse. I didn't know any of them well, and I have no idea what was actually passing through their minds. I assumed at the time that they knew I was dying. I might already be dead. That's what I understood of the situation, and if something was so obvious a child could see it, surely the adults knew it too. The oil felt cool on my fevered scalp. They said a prayer I didn't understand, and I fell to sleep. All I could smell was the sourness of hot and sweaty skin. I survived, but I still remember the scene, the cool oil, and the smell of fever.

A decade or so later, after a rocky start, I dove into my mission work in southern Louisiana with gusto. Within a month or two, I ended up on splits with a senior companion in an unfamiliar area, on one of the hot nights that seep out of the wet Louisiana soil. We had an appointment, I discovered, to minister to a woman dying of liver failure. I remember little of that night, except that the senior companion knew what death smelled like. He told me so, with the nonchalant superiority of a twenty-year-old boy. Impending death was by far the strongest smell in that room. It took me months, if not years, to understand that there was another, more earnest and hopeful, scent present as well: warm olive oil on mortal skin.

I encountered this oil again as a young father, another decade or so later. My second daughter, barely four, had croup, that terrifying inflammation of the top of the windpipe that makes the sound of fearful frogs when the child tries to breathe. She was exhausted, and so was I.

I asked her if she would like a blessing. I explained that I would anoint her head with olive oil, the fruits of the earth once used by the Hebrews to crown kings. I told her I would then "seal" her blessing. She and her sister asked what it meant to seal, and I explained that it was a special kind of prayer, one that recognized how much like Jesus she was. She smiled to hear that Jesus had another name ("Christ") that meant that he was anointed, just as she would be. Her face lightened as she considered my proposal. She consented, with a nod.

I dabbed a drop of oil on the crown of her head, just enough that she could feel its cool presence on her scalp. As I placed my hands onto her head, touching the drop of oil lightly, she held out her right hand, stroking my forearm with her small fingers. The tang of olive oil mixed with hair settled, permanently, into my memory as the olfactory mark of my approach to God's presence.

I knew that she would improve, that the course of viral infections is almost always benign. But I wanted her to know that she was loved by Heavenly and earthly parents, and I wanted to share my faith in God with her. After the blessing she nestled in my armpit and wrapped an arm around my stomach as she settled, reassured, into sleep.

After my wife taught me to cook, I came to know olive oil in its many strains and variations. I began to understand how the volatile remnants of the lives of the olives give the oil complexity and enhance the pleasure on our tongues. I love culinary oil and am delighted when a friend gives us a bottle of the good stuff, still bursting with the flavors of the patch of earth where its tree placed its roots. But there is nothing for me like the scent of oil on skin, that lucid mixture of earthly and divine that calls us into the life of God.

These smells are memories and histories. They are the many days we have spent together in tenderness. They are also the promise of what we hope will one day take place. I pray that when the day comes to fall at the feet of the One who tread the winepress alone that I will recognize him. That I will see him as the one anointed for eternity with the oil pressed from the fruit of Gethsemane's trees. I pray that he will sense a hint of that sacred scent lingering in my too-human heart. Because I belong to him in that same heart and that same garden.

PART THREE:
THE SCRIPTURES

Who's My David?

We were sitting in Sunday School, my oldest daughter and I, listening to a lesson on the David and Goliath story (see 1 Samuel 17). It's one of the stories that established David as the rightful king of Israel because he—a mere shepherd boy—vanquished the Philistines' mighty warrior, Goliath. This colossal man from the town of Gath stood, according to the Bible account, over nine feet tall. He wore armor that easily weighed as much as the wispy David, Jesse's youngest son, who was too slight to have been deployed in battle. Goliath the giant taunted the Israelites, saying they could stop the destruction of war in a moment if they advanced a champion who could best him in hand-to-hand combat. No Israelite came forward until God guided David to the field of battle. God blessed David with the extraordinary power to vanquish the mighty, armored giant. He threw a stone from his sling, striking Goliath in the open space in his helmet. Israel won the war, and David moved toward his destiny as king. The battle between David and Goliath is an exciting story that we might recognize today in the long conflict between Harry Potter and Voldemort in J. K.

Rowling's fantasy books. In honesty, this story of David and Goliath has been retold in thousands of variations. There's a reason we love these stories of victorious underdogs: we imagine that we are the underdog, and we expect that we will one day win.

We as a Sunday School class settled into the story as a group of underdogs hoping to prevail against monstrous opponents. "Who is your Goliath?" the teacher asked. A man told the story of his struggle with drug addiction and the petty crime that supported it. His Goliath was drug addiction, and God had filled his sling with the stone of sobriety. Others had similar, if less dramatic, stories to tell. We had all overcome challenges and resisted the cruelly powerful.

The familiar rhythms of the lesson drew me toward my usual absentmindedness. Then my daughter turned to me and asked, "Dad, who's your Goliath? Probably [name redacted]," naming a man at work who had caused me substantial heartache over the years. He'd brought about enough pain that my daughter knew him by name. Yes, I thought, if I wanted to be melodramatic about it. He is my Goliath, the eight-hundred-pound gorilla of a Philistine that disrupts my professional life. She paused then, in the way she does when she's about to change my understanding of the world. "Wait," she said, something bothering her about the traditional framing of the problem. "Are you *his* Goliath?"

I lost my breath. She'd stolen the smug quiet of my story about this poisonous work relationship. She had immediately reconfigured the story of this man's life and my intersections with it. I realized, ruefully, that I have almost certainly caused this man great pain. I had stomped my giant, armor-clad body before him and waved my sword, mocking his fear.

Her comment and the subsequent realization brought to mind my many Davids over the years. In my life, the clearest memory of that realization was my walk of reconciliation just after my freshman year of college. As I've mentioned, I had only been converted to belief in God a few weeks before I left for school, and the remorseful work of repentance was not far off. I realized that in my decade of defensive and angry atheism, I had not only shoplifted or vandalized (which required financial compensation) but had been cruel.

I especially realized that my ninth-grade chemistry teacher, Mr. S, had been my David. I think I immediately intuited that he wasn't confident in his work on the first day of class. I rapidly saw myself as knowing more chemistry than he did. In retrospect, he was the person in authority who was weakest, so I latched onto him as an easy target. I think I explained my behavior to myself as a necessary corrective to the unrighteous dominion of those in power. I think I also loved the positive attention from the other students when I mocked and disrespected this man. My mother told me that he cried in mute rage during a parent-teacher conference with her. At the time I took his characterization of me as the worst student he'd ever taught as a compliment. It was like getting the blue ribbon for arrogance at the state fair.

So, in the full itinerary of paying for items shoplifted, returning what had been taken, and begging forgiveness, I found my way to Mr. S's classroom. He was packing his teaching materials into boxes. He remembered me, and I could see that he wasn't quite sure how to respond to my presence in his professional space. He still winced at the sight of me.

As I explained to him how sorry I was, his eyes misted with tears. He explained that he was retiring that year from teaching and that the thing that had made sense of a career of struggles was the hope that his students would turn out to be decent human beings. My penitence helped to prove to him that his work had not been in vain. Without trying to claim an importance that does not belong to me, I think that God wanted me in that school on that day so that Mr. S's life story could include the confidence that he had shaped the souls of adolescents. However bad I had been, on that day I was good.

In light of my daughter's view of Goliath, I look back on that story with new perspective. God knew I was Goliath. God had called me to take off my armor, to expose the soft parts of my frame, and make peace with the Israelites.

Of course, fickle human that I am, by the time of our David and Goliath discussion in Sunday School, I'd forgotten the lesson I thought I had learned with Mr. S and his chemistry classroom. I hadn't returned to the buffoonish cruelty of my youth, but I had forgotten to keep my eye out for the Davids on my journey. Like a dog to its own vomit, as the book of Proverbs (26:11) likes to scold, I had become Goliath again. That insight troubled me deeply. I felt the need to repent again.

Since my daughter's reproof, I've begun a new spiritual practice. When I start to think I've encountered a Goliath in my life, I pause now and ask whether I am in fact the Goliath. Sometimes I really am a David of sorts. Sometimes I'm honestly and fairly pursuing an important and worthy objective, and someone stands gloomily in the path. In that case, I carry on. Life has such moments, and we must, selectively and circumspectly, be able to choose the right and let the consequences follow. But most of the time I am, when I take stock of the situation, a nine-foot Philistine warrior wearing heavy armor and waving my giant sword in a young shepherd's face. (I find that I must also ask myself the Goliath question when I feel like I'm getting my way in a controversy or dispute.) This is painful and hard work. It's much easier to press on with routine tasks.

I know that some people, including people I love and admire, use similar tactics to advocate for moral relativism in our modern culture wars. I hear and honor the love of the vulnerable that drives so much of their resistance to the generations that came before us. But I haven't found that this new spiritual practice has changed my attachment to truth, beauty, and goodness. I'm not saying that there is no truth or that anything anyone happens to say from some hidden "authentic" core of their personality is the truth, even for them. Instead I'm trying to exercise Christian humility. I'm trying to see the world the way God does. In this case, the mandate from God does share practical implications with some of the calls for greater respect for people who have been historically marginalized, and it's good that it does. Here the Bible provides an opportunity to celebrate a shared belief, in the face of theological differences, even as it unsettles the automatic notion that we are all always Davids.

As I practice this Christian humility inspired by reading the David and Goliath story upside down, I find myself a more civil, careful, and thoughtful opponent. When I must overrule the wishes of another, I disagree with a heavier heart than I used to, and with an earnest straining to understand how the world looks across the table. I'm far from perfect and am aware that I will still be Goliath to some people some of the time. But I'm trying to be less the military figure enamored of his own strength and more the tiny adolescent called by God. And I owe that insight to a young woman, a Sunday School class, and the soulful inversion of an old Bible story.

Suffer the Children

By inclination, I'm something of a misanthrope. I'm not sure where I came by this trait. Maybe it's good old-fashioned nature, some mixture of a thousand different genes that makes me by default uninterested in other human beings. Maybe I've got something wrong with my hippocampus or superior temporal sulcus, too many or too few synapses in my brain. As a teenager, I wondered whether I was a (nonviolent, noncriminal) sociopath because I felt so little engaged in the world of people. That imaginary pathology was more impressive than thinking that I was shy, self-absorbed, and socially clumsy. If I'd been born in the 1990s rather than the '70s, I would have placed myself on the autism spectrum instead. With time, I came to see this alienation as a badge of honor. I was authentically alone, like Albert Camus wandering the bars of Paris, and what the world did with my alienation was no concern of mine.

Nurture has a claim here, too, I'm sure. I grew up in a smoldering train wreck of a childhood. I spent over a decade wishing for a father who was more than a donor of genes and fantasizing about some modicum of financial security. I was ashamed of our poverty and weakness; I knew that other families were better than ours. We didn't belong. I don't really fault my younger self for suspecting the motives and even the relevance of others. My early experience with people was often deeply disappointing.

It didn't help, I suspect, that I'm physically inclined to live inside my head. If I had my inborn druthers, I'd spend my waking hours reading, writing, and thinking. When hunger struck, I would eat, book in hand, oblivious to the world of humans, then fall asleep with the book laid open over my face.

But I haven't had those druthers, and that, as the Northeastern folk poet said, has made all the difference.

Not long after my mission, I found myself drawn back to my native alienation. It's been a constant struggle for me to inhabit the world of people. I've had moments, even months, of warm clarity of vision. But then I have receded again into my natural state, bondage to some vision of my own power and priority. My wife and then my children, in company with others who have loved me, have slowly made me more open and tender—even loving. By the time I was in my thirties, I still struggled with the nagging sense that I was by nature a misanthrope. But there were people in my life whom I loved, and I could generally be kind to the rest, as long as I remembered to work at it.

Still, whatever peace I had made with adults, I remained mystified by, even terrified of, children other than my own. People laugh at me to hear this confession, and they probably should. I am laughable. But there was the reality of it: I was afraid of children. They were urgent babblers who spewed syllables and body fluids like tiny volcanos of mucus, vinegar, and baking soda. Their ways were not mine. Perhaps, although I wasn't open to the idea at the time, they reminded me of my own childhood weakness and pain. Whatever the reason, I maintained a wary distance. Even my own children, whom I loved deeply as people, mystified me in their childness.

Then my wife fell ill when we turned forty, and her sickness turned my world upside down. Absent my cool detachment and comfortable smugness, I was brutally, ruthlessly exposed to the elements, like a mountaineer wearing swim trunks on the upper slopes of Mount Everest. I had lost my protective indifference to the world in its terrible beauty and disorienting mysteries. I finally realized, in retrospect, that my lifelong habit of misanthropy was born of fear.

Neither nature nor nurture, the alliterative pillars of determinism, were adequate when put to the test in my life. They said little of any significance about substantive human problems. I yearned for something more than just the endowments of nature and nurture, something more than the asphyxiating cocoon I'd spun around myself in protective denial of the world outside my head. I found myself needing to rest on the twin pillars of a different faith than physical determinism. I needed real choice, and I needed Christ. The "authentic," misanthropic self that nature and nurture had bestowed on me was useless. If anything, that self clouded my vision. I chose instead to try to make myself open to the mind of Christ.

My lifelong disdain didn't belong in this new phase of life. God had not called me to aloof indifference toward children. I could do better. I needed to see more clearly. In Matthew 19, in the midst of some hard preaching, the crowds bring their children in the hopes that Jesus will bless them with health and safety by placing his hands on their heads. The disciples, protecting their weary leader, "rebuke" the hopeful parents. Jesus, once again pointing out the blindness of his disciples, says, "Suffer little children, and forbid them not, to come unto me: for of such is the kingdom of heaven" (Matthew 19:14). He then blesses the children. This tiny story is one of many telling the core witness of the New Testament: the disciples are blind, and the people we are prone to overlook are the most important citizens of God's kingdom. In my early fear of children, I was the typical disciple until Jesus led me to allow the children to come, and to see that they are heaven's own.

While I don't think of myself as possessing spiritual gifts, I am able to elucidate subtle connections through persistent questioning. I've used this ability to good effect in my scientific and historical writing. I hadn't, though, asked too many questions about my trademark cynicism. I started to really wonder how the world might look to God, especially the human part of it that still frightened me.

I began a spiritual discipline. I asked myself to imagine how children might look to God—luminous bundles of grace with their mortal lives waiting to happen, free as yet from world weariness. I took the time to smile at the kids at church and in the neighborhood. And I allowed myself to be more vulnerable to human goodness that was not mediated by high culture or scholarly sophistication. I worked to attend to flowers and clouds and laughing faces. I struggled to spend a little more time outside my head each day. This spiritual practice (and the divine power that motivated it) began, over the course of some months, to shape me.

Then one day in church I found myself cradling a friend's infant son on my lap as we both half dozed to the rhythms of a slow Sunday School lesson. I was holding him to give my friends a break from the constant effort of early parenthood. This baby boy had big eyes bursting with wonder and thin hair that stretched in every direction. He seemed ready to eat the world in one giant swallow.

I discovered that something had changed in me. It was as if I'd awakened, startled, from a half-remembered dream. I realized in that moment that I had learned to love children. Not just my own children. But the whole motley crowd of weak and insistent babblers. They were my people too.

I'm different these days. I smile at the sight of a baby, which genuinely cheers me. I don't mind babysitting. I enjoy chatting with small children and even interact occasionally with teenagers. I find that my love for my own children has deepened. And I feel ever more distant from the younger me who wondered whether he was congenitally unable to participate in the lives of others.

The scholar in me notes that there's nothing authentic about this spiritual discipline and its outcomes. This kindness to children is not a native part of my life or personality. It's as strange to me as walking on my hands instead of my feet. However genuine it has become, this goodness is something I had to choose despite myself, over my authentic objections. If someone wanted to attach this new trait to nature or nurture, we'd have to bypass more than four decades of my mortal life to imagine some late-onset genetic disorder or some Manchurian Candidate of childhood trauma just waiting for a specific environmental trigger to call it forth. I suppose we could stretch the facts to make that work, but such explanations strain credulity on scientific and religious grounds. I don't doubt that these recent experiences and the reconfiguration of my soul are mediated in part by biology and history. Of course they are. I'm mortal, after all. I'm just not gullible enough to think that there's nothing more to it than that. I think this is what the early Christians understood as the new life from above, the changed soul that is in Christ. The Greek term for it, *metanoia*, is only partly captured by our word "repentance." This I think is one vista onto losing your life to find it again.

Nor does the modern aesthetic of authenticity shed any special light here. By the lights of authenticity, I'm an aloof intellectual who has little time for others. I'm natively impatient and more than a little blind to what is good and beautiful. This love of the strange simplicity of children feels as familiar as breathing to me now, but it's not authentic. Not remotely. Instead, it's the sweet fruit of spiritual practice in an orchard I had to plant and till and sweat over. I'm not dimwitted enough to claim that I am the sole or even primary reason this tree has grown and borne fruit. But I know that this specific fruit in this specific life required that I choose to deviate from the authentic life I received from nature, nurture, and history.

I know that I come across as sentimental now. I've become a subject better fit for Hallmark cards than the strenuous realities of our cutthroat economic systems. I still feel the occasional pang of self-consciousness when I realize how soft-hearted I've become. Sometimes I miss the strength I perceived in protective indifference. Then I realize that aloof skepticism for all those years stole from me the holy proximity of other people. I know how little the youthful me would admire this turn into weakness. But this new world is where divine love has drawn me, and in this vulnerability stands the possibility of a life beyond my former authenticity.

And thank God for this surprising grace, this yearning to see in love, and the influence of these young people. Suffer the children, indeed.

Your Socks
Don't Match

The account of the paralyzed man in John 5 is a dead-serious joke pretending to be a simple story. It's easy to miss the humor, especially in the King James translation. But slow the story down, walk it through its paces, and it's insightfully, delightfully absurd.

There's a pool near the Sheep Gate in Jerusalem. Its precise name is lost to history, but we are accustomed to calling it Bethsaida. Whatever the original name, it's a healing pool, and tradition holds that right after the pool seems to boil, the first person to enter its healing waters receives the greatest portion of restored health. Angels, it turns out, are the cause of those bubbles, stirring the pool with their otherworldly power.[1]

A man at this pool has been known to have a neurological disorder that has prevented him from walking for thirty-eight

---

1. Thomas Wayment notes in *The New Testament: A Translation for Latter-day Saints* (Provo, UT: Religious Studies Center, Brigham Young University; Salt Lake City: Deseret Book, 2019), 174, that the phrase "waiting for the moving of water" in John 5:3 is "added by some late and inferior Greek manuscripts to the end of this verse. The addition is unlikely to be original to the Fourth Gospel."

years. He lies at the angelic waters day after day, praying that just once he might be able to get into the pool first to access its healing power. But every time the waters bubble, the healthier people—those whose afflictions don't limit their ability to get in and out of the pool—jump in before he can enter. The disabled man is living an ancient version of the catch-22. The only way to be healed is to be well enough to jump into the pool before anyone else does.

Then comes Jesus. He notices the man beside the pool and asks him his story. We wonder whether this is the first time anyone has really noticed the man in his decades as a troubling presence beside the troubled waters. When Jesus hears the terrible story of others walking over the disabled man in the interests of achieving their own healing, the Messiah circumvents the entire twisted system. He heals the man then and there, without requiring a visit to the pool. Pick up your mattress and walk, he says. Forget about the crass jostling in the lines that form beside the pool. Welcome to a new life.

The disabled man—wondering, I suspect, why he spent years sitting beside a pool that wasn't necessary after all—stands, picks up his dingy, flimsy bed, and walks away from the pool. For the first time in thirty-eight years, he is moving under the power of his own limbs. This is astounding news. One imagines defiant joy on his face as his legs first start their work. One imagines him wanting to abandon that reminder of his vulnerability, the portable bed he has lain on all these years. But perhaps the burden of these many years of poverty is not so quick to leave him.

Why didn't he just leave his mat there? Was it to avoid littering? Was it the only bed his poverty allowed, necessary for him to sleep that night? Was it for the brilliant incongruity of walking while carrying a beggar's pallet, the bulky emblem of his prior physical disability? Or was it just that Jesus's instructions had been to pick up his mattress and walk? We don't know and won't ever know in mortality. But that was the scene presented to observers. A miracle had happened in the tatters of a life of physical desperation. Both man and mattress are now vertical rather than horizontal.

A group of pious Judeans stops the newly ambulating man because, they explain, he is carrying his bed on a Saturday.[2] Moving furniture, as all secular work, violates Israel's covenantal obligation to honor God's Sabbath. The man responds—almost like Adam trying to throw Eve under the bus when the pair are caught newly wise and clothed in the Garden of Eden—that a healer told him to do so. His Judean critics then try to identify the mysterious healer who told the man to violate the sabbath. We are drawn into this cat-and-mouse story and wonder where it will end up, even as we wonder how it is that those Judeans don't already know that the healer is Jesus. We are poised to see those Judeans as keystone cops, bumbling in attempts to find their suspect, our hero in hiding.

Step back from this story a few paces, though. A man who has been paralyzed for nearly four decades is suddenly able to walk, and the first thing that comes to the minds of the Judean observers is that he is breaking a rule about carrying furniture? Really? They seem blind to the miracle of his ability to carry his mattress in the first place. Dwell with the absurdity for a moment. It's like discovering that a friend has been raised from the dead and noticing only that his socks don't match. There are bigger issues at play than fashion sense when the dead rise.

We need to understand what was going on in times of the New Testament. The people in power fought Jesus tooth and nail and finally executed him. They were blind to his glory and his mission. They were truly clueless. This joke about those Judeans and the man healed must have had the early Chris-

---

2. The KJV translates *Ioudaioi* in John 5 as "Jews"; N. T Wright translates the term as "Judeans" in *The Kingdom New Testament: A Contemporary Translation* (New York: HarperCollins, 2011).

tians in stitches. It wasn't that those Judeans were "Jewish"—
many Christians were Jewish too, for heaven's sake. But the
Judeans in John 5 were powerful, and they were blind to the
majesty of heaven and earth.

Gospel jokes have more work to do than the jokes that
just pass the time or brighten a night out with friends. Non-
gospel humor plays with expectations and moral intuitions to
see whether we can be surprised in a merry or sarcastic way.
Gospel jokes, especially in scripture, happily surprise us with
incongruity or absurdity. But they also drive us to be better, to
be spiritually renewed, as we laugh. In this case, the joke is on
us. The story of the encounter between the Judean critics and
the healed man carrying the emblem of his prior disability in
violation of Sabbath rules sees our hearts and exposes what
we dare not see. We are, far too often, as blind as those smug
Judeans were. We are prone to complain to the resurrected
that their socks don't match.

I'm as guilty as the rest. While I'm not as concerned about
questions of traditional piety, I have my own trivial bundle of
prejudices. I don't like nonethnic body art, skinny jeans, pop
psychology, or talking to pets. I'm vaguely afraid of cowboys
and construction workers, and I don't like expensive clothing,
politicians, or men with southern accents. I suspect that my
list is no more or less laughable than anyone else's irrational
prejudices. I'm not proud of the list. I just notice it by way of
confession.

More than I care to admit, I'm an upscale Judean looking
down my nose at the Sabbath-breaking mattress when I meet
someone who pushes my buttons. My mind starts to drift, or
I struggle to take the person seriously. Your accent makes you
seem stupid; your shirt's too expensive; your tattoo is taw-
dry. Those are the horrid thoughts that periodically percolate.
Reading John 5 as sharply funny taught me that I was being
blind about my prejudices. Note my sin. Here I am standing
in front of a vessel of divine grace, a human tangle of flesh,

bones, and neurons that can speak and dream, wonder and love. And my eyes are drawn to some ink marks on the skin. *You're moving furniture on the Sabbath*, I seem to be saying to a paralyzed man walking by. *What's wrong with you?* But the joke's on me.

I'm not the only one with this problem. We're all prone to miss the point, sometimes catastrophically. Sometimes smoking is the sin that distracts us from seeing the true glory of people and the world in which they dwell; sometimes it is that they seem too pious or naïve. Sometimes we get distracted by the color of their skin or their beliefs about how human sexuality ought to be understood. We all have our list of prejudgments that blind us.

C. S. Lewis captured the basic sentiment in a famous phrase. "It is a serious thing to live in a society of possible gods and goddesses," he says. He's right. We are surrounded by vast and powerful beings who will soon be substantially divine even if their humanity seems too much to us at a given moment. As a Latter-day Saint, I have to believe that these people who surround me are already divine at some level and always have been. It's not that they will be glorious at some far distant time when we will all be unrecognizably superior. It's that they are already marvels of divine power.

The laugh is on me when I get distracted by body art or the smell of tobacco smoke on an old shirt. I'm as obtuse as those Judeans looking at the man's mattress, blind to the fact that a paralyzed person is ambling past them under his own power. I'm inclined to squabble with my youngest daughter— bright and kind and independent and impulsive and sometimes a bit wild, the way I was as an adolescent—a little too often. I'm working now to return my mind consistently to the fact that she is a goddess. I ask myself in a given circumstance whether I'm complaining about unmatched socks or moving furniture on a Sunday. Every time, I realize that I'm committing the sins of the critical fat cats in John 5. Sure, she is breaking a rule here or there—screen time limits or rules of civil conversation—and rules ought to be obeyed. But she is a stunning miracle, an expression of the grand beauty that God has loved into the world and the divinity of each of us. I have in the past forgotten those facts at my peril. I have cut myself off from the gospel message brought into the world in Jesus's ministry. I'm working now to celebrate the miracles that otherwise evade my vision.

Since delving into John 5 for a neighborhood Bible study and discovering its brilliant and painful humor, I've been experimenting with a spiritual practice meant to defend against this strain of blindness. I've begun to coach myself to call the people I encounter "goddesses" and "gods." I can't transform every encounter every day into something beyond human expression. I am mortal, and mortals are often blind and sullen. I struggle sometimes under the pretentious weight of this practice. And yet I try to align myself with that marvelous reality by remembering.

What of the Wisdom of Solomon?

'm one of the adult Sunday School teachers in my ward and began to serve in that calling during an Old Testament year. Coming to the text again after many years of neglect, I found the Bible a much livelier read than I had before. It was still a strange collection of books, but it was also packed with soulful stories that sometimes crackled with the divine presence. This was especially true when we stumbled into the seemingly endless annals of the kings of Israel and Judah in Kings and Samuel.

In our attempt to make some sense of the first few chapters of 1 Kings, we focused on the famous story about Solomon's ability to see to the heart of a dispute between two women over their infant sons, one dead and the other alive (see 1 Kings 3:16–28). Solomon's famous proposal to cut the live boy into two pieces immediately identified the true mother. I've always loved the story as an elegant judicial tactic that shone a light on the dark corners of human nature. For me, the focus of the story was on Solomon and his actions. It was a compelling account of supernaturally wise jurisprudence in ancient Israel.

In retrospect, I had no idea what was going on in this story. Not really. It wasn't until I returned to that makeshift courtroom as an adult, preparing a Sunday School lesson, that I began to see the encounter in a new and holy light.

Some basic details about the text and its probable history is enough to orient ourselves to the biblical situation. Solomon was not the one of King David's sons that was expected to succeed him. His elder brother Adonijah had claimed that honor. Instead, the prophet Nathan and Solomon's mother, probably Bathsheba, exploited the failing wits of the second king of united Israel, her addled but still powerful husband, David. After the queen's careful coordination and with the backing of the prophet, Solomon's chances for succession looked pretty good.

As it happens, Solomon did assume the throne, but his reign was to be short-lived unless he consolidated power, rapidly. He did so by systematically executing anyone who might make a claim to his throne or be a key supporter of any other contender. Solomon's early reign is a brutal chronicle, not for the faint of heart. These are old stories about vulnerable rulers and their fractious successors that we'll recognize from a thousand other traditions.

This was ancient Israel, though. It wasn't enough to be powerful and to kill off your enemies. A king also had to wield the wisdom of Jehovah. Solomon had consolidated his power, but he had yet to demonstrate that God had endowed him with divine wisdom.

Into this fraught moment in the reign of Israel's third king walk two angry, fearful, grief-stricken prostitutes. Roommates, they lived on the tattered edges of a society that cared about them only to the extent they could sell their sexual intimacy to incontinent men. Both had infant sons. Both had awakened that morning to discover their boy was dead (the first one to awaken swapped her dead baby for the other's live one before the second awoke to the sight of that same dead baby beneath her breast). The living son's fate was the judicial problem to test the new king—which woman could rightfully claim the boy? In Israelite law at the time, only men could provide testimony in court. Given the lack of men to resolve the issues or provide reliable testimony (their world was not ours, and it placed women in much worse positions than we would now tolerate), the decision of which woman would claim the baby depended on the intervention of a wise judge. If God in fact favored him, Solomon was such a man. Now is the moment to understand whether God really had blessed Solomon with wisdom.

The testimony begins with a woman declaring that the other woman had stolen her live son while she slept. She testifies at length, indicating that her son was older by three days and confirming that there was no man in the house who might adjudicate the legal question. Many scholars think that Solomon quickly figured out that the woman who spoke first about death (for example, her baby died, mine survived) was the one whose baby had actually died. The one who began her declarations with life (for example, my baby lives, her baby died) was the one whose baby was still alive. They're probably right: ancient Hebrew readers and writers often saw the order of words and clauses as containing meanings that escape our American English attention. So, after noticing that distinction in speech patterns between the two women, Solomon apparently knows the answer to the puzzle.

But in the absence of legally permissible testimony, a test is necessary to prove the truth to the court and the nation. Solomon knows what happened, in other words, but he has to demonstrate it. So, he proposes to treat the baby as a piece of inanimate property that could easily be split to share it between the two women, like a contested bushel of barley or a pail of sheep milk. The frightened mother of the live boy exclaims that she would rather see her son raised by her roommate than see him dead. The bereaved mother of the dead boy falls into Solomon's trap and asks for her half of the surviving boy.

What possible sense could this dilemma make as Solomon posed it? Better my child be dead than taken from me? I don't know any parents who believe that, unless they have actually lost their mind. But wait. Maybe what Solomon has done here is allowed us a sideways glance into the minds and motivations of these two women. One is bereaved to the point of insanity. The other is apprehensive and upset but secure in the knowledge that her son is alive. In other words, what if this test is intended to determine which of the women is truly broken by grief?

While, due to anxiety I've suffered over the years, I've lived through the loss of my children in panicked daydreams many times, my children have only ever suffered one actual medical problem, which responded well to treatment, however terrifying the path to diagnosis was. I know and love, however, a handful of people who have suffered precisely that most terrible of all bereavements. That grief breaks the soul; it tears words from throats and ransacks minds. There is perhaps no grief greater than that of a parent whose young child has died.

And now I find myself struck with godly sorrow. What I thought was a story about a wise man exposing a criminal is actually a story about a desolate mother whose grief has carried her beyond sanity. I've had to confess that in the past I judged the bereaved mother as a jealous woman who hated her roommate and wanted to steal another woman's baby in order to hide a negligent infanticide. I was dead wrong.

Instead, now I see the annihilating scream of a woman all alone, mentally broken by the realization that she accidentally smothered her child. I suppose it's useful to understand the way that Solomon got to the nature of that soul-breaking grief in his famous thought experiment. I guess it's helpful to know that this feat (and presumably others like it) clinched Solomon's authority as the king chosen by God for Israel. But those political facts pale in comparison with the enormous, feral anguish of a mother who blames herself for her baby's death. That seems to me to be the stunning display, the outpouring of insight, from this passage in 1 Kings 3.

We have seen into the heart of this young mother, brutally alone in her grief. But what do we do next? Do we think, as my young self did, "Great work, Detective Solomon: you solved the case"? Or do we ask, "O God, how can we be vessels of healing for this grief-ruptured woman?" Such a stark view into the heart of another person is an obligation. It's a covenant, not a titillation. Solomon's court is no reality TV show, in which voyeurs bask in the misery of hapless defendants. It is a Christian call to love, prayer, and action. It is a revelation. So here I stand, heartbroken and renewed not so much by the wisdom of Solomon as by the covenantal obligation that another's grief imposes on me. The tears of the grief-mad woman flow from the waters in which I was baptized (see Mosiah 18:8–9). I cannot refuse to see them.

From this story I have come to see an obligation to love those who are grief-stricken. The fact of the obligation seems clear. What we haven't really understood is what that obligation might look like. This is a delicate and vastly important dance to which we God-loving mortals are called. Real and overwhelming grief had overtaken the bereaved woman. That is perfectly and painfully true. She believed that she needed to steal her roommate's child and possibly condemn him to death. Within her soul, a horrible, actual grief thus merged with a false belief that threatened to compound her pain.

My wife, ever wise, wondered to me whether perhaps Solomon proposed the solution he did—cutting the baby in half and giving equal parts to the two mothers—as a way to draw to the surface the internal state of the mourning mother. Reading the story from her own generous, Christian perspective, my wife thought that the young but wise king proposed the death of the child so that he could help the grief-stricken mother confront a false and terrible belief. She had come to see herself as a killer of children. She had accidentally smothered her child in her sleep. Now, with her response to Solomon's terrible decree, she seemed to be saying that she was the kind of person who kills children. In desperate fatalism, she concluded that she would kill again. That's who she was, she thought. Nothing could be done about it. My wife saw that by calling out the truth and handing the baby over to its biological mother, Solomon was saying to the bereaved woman, "You are not a murderer of children." I don't know whether that's what actually ran through Solomon's mind, but I love this image and the possibilities it evokes. Our obligation in the face of grief is clear and weighty; the way to honor the covenantal obligation to the griever will require spirit, wisdom, and grace. Sometimes, perhaps often, it will require that we gesture in love toward a path beyond false beliefs.

In mourning with those who mourn, in being God's arms wrapped around the sufferer's shoulders, we must be filled with God's love. That does not mean we should be blind to reality. In fact, love may require that we work together to see clearly. We all of us have lapses of vision; grief and mental illness may especially threaten our sight.

The specific problem of the bereaved mother is a vexing and important one for us now. The warping of her soul by grief knew only that grief, which followed an internal mandate to spread outward—misery too often begets misery. What mattered most to her in this blinding sorrow was that her roommate should know the same sorrow. If she had to lose her son, why shouldn't this other mother?

And here we start to grapple more straightforwardly with an increasing problem for us today. The Bible's compilers—concerned more with proving that Solomon rather than Adonijah was the rightful heir to Israel's throne—had no interest in the next and harder phase of responding to tragedy.

The Bible story ends with Solomon's detective work deciding the fate of the live boy.

But what about the dead boy and his bereaved mother? How should we honor and engage her pain without capitulating to either her need to make the world miserable, or society's apparent need to imagine that her misery must not exist? In her misery's madness, she had wanted the world to look as bleak as her pain. Society just wanted her out of their sight. What decent person would care about sex workers and their illegitimate children, I can imagine them asking.

Between those two extremes is where we must steer our vessels. The world continues full of suffering. We in modern culture stretch ourselves to limit cruelty and to hear the voices of those who have been pushed aside or who are now ignored, disrespected, or even terrorized. As we do so—following thereby the clear and overwhelming message of the New Testament and restored gospel—the story of the grief-stricken mother calls us to look closer. Sometimes, perhaps often, our love will need to feel passionately and to think clearly, to call into true communion rather than merely resonate with anger or mental illness. We may be prone to love too little or to love too much.

God is glad when we are smart or wise as Solomon was. But God cares more whether we can see with clarity and love into the broken heart of a sufferer. And whether from that sight come acts of healing care.

Achieving the godly balance of a love that is neither too little nor too much is more complicated than could be fit into an instruction manual. But we can recognize that balance when we watch carefully. I see the importance of this balance in current conversations about grievance and trauma. We can respond to these reports by saying that it's all in their minds, that the sufferer needs to just "get over it." Or we can agree with the sufferer that the misery they experienced will define them forever. Neither of these extremes is likely to communicate divine love—we will need to locate places of grace between those two poles. Finding such places takes careful work: our response to others' pain will require patient trial and error. We would be well served to pray for the compassionate wisdom of Solomon and then ask ourselves some questions. How much is this encounter about me rather than the sufferer? What feelings am I experiencing, and are they blurring my vision? How much time am I willing to take to get this right? Does the fate of the sufferer matter to me?

I've witnessed this problem at a minor level in my own family. Over the years, I've watched my daughters fight, especially as they entered their teen years. I suspect that they never fought any more than other siblings, but the conflicts have felt very real to them. At the peak of battle, they would come to me to adjudicate their grievances. They wanted me, they shouted across each other, to decide who was right and who was wrong. My response at the time was to tell them that they could and should solve the problem on their own. They would be better off resolving their controversies without adult input. I pretended to myself that I wanted them to grow in discernment and independence. But they knew I was lying at least to myself and probably to them as well. I was refusing to participate in their lives at times of passionate need. On the surface, I was a tempered, rational father, but in my heart I lacked the wisdom of Solomon. I didn't jump angrily into the fray, true, but my aloofness was its own form of betrayal. I'm trying now to see with wiser eyes, to care enough to see. I owe it to the bereaved mother, whose heart was made visible in the court of Solomon.

PART FOUR:
WORSHIP

Promises to Keep

We kneel across the altar from each other. I see her face; how different it is now. It's more familiar to me than any other. I know that face everywhere and anywhere. Friends say she looks the same as she did when we met, but I know better. I've watched her features every day. I like the way they age, even as I know how fragile our bodies are. These bodies have forbidden us to forget their transience. I know that as I hold her hand across the altar.

We are getting ritually married in a Latter-day Saint temple on behalf of a couple from seventeenth-century Europe whose French-sounding names the kindly old man who is acting as sealer can barely pronounce. One of them he spells instead of speaking, in weary frustration.

I remember two decades ago, when we knelt across a similar altar for our own wedding. I don't remember much of our first time at the altar other than my overwhelming fear. I couldn't bear the thought then of getting married, but I loved her and wanted to share our lives. The first year of marriage was as miserable as you'd expect from a groom who almost fainted from anxiety, dithering about whether to flee his own nuptials. (She had her own serious reservations that day, she likes to remind me. Several of her friends were astounded that we finished the ceremony without getting the paramedics involved. We were both as gray as wet paper.)

It took years for us to find our rhythm together. I was arrogant and distant and thought domestic work was beneath me. I did "important" things instead. After a few childless years, we went on to have three daughters. Parenthood was typically hard. We had lovely and beloved children and the usual time constraints peculiar to that phase of life. We had our squabbles and petty resentments, exhaustion—about what you'd expect from parenting with a half-committed husband. Sometimes life stretched us dangerously thin.

Now we are sealing a child to parents, an analogue to marriage that binds children to parents for eternity. An older man from the neighborhood drapes his hand over ours, his skin wrinkled and his thumb joint bent by advanced arthritis. He smiles. I can see in his face that this is serious business. With our bodies serving as ritual objects, a man is bound to his parents in eternity. He too lived in seventeenth-century Europe. These are the people whose stories are intertwining with ours.

I love this moment. I cherish the idea that we are connected and connecting. I admire the loose skin covering this older brother's deforming joints. I appreciate that the generations have been reversed as a man older than our parents is standing in for a son lost to the centuries. I treasure the fact that my wife and I have been allowed to grow two decades older together and that I have become her helpmeet. It's hard work, sometimes desperate work. Tears of sadness, frustration, or pain still sometimes fall. We have consecrated the work, the sadness, and the sanctity to being and growing together.

I've never been good about wearing my wedding ring. The original one was a gold alloy band from the 1960s, the remnant of my mother-in-law's failed marriage. She divorced the father-in-law I never met for sleeping with his secretary. My wife was six weeks old when he left. There's no time like pregnancy, I suppose, for adultery. If one must betray, one may as well do it horrifically. He took his own life a decade or so later. I wonder whether he remembered that gold band, that precious daughter, as he made his final preparations. My own father's infidelity was another gruesome tale that ended in premature death, less clearly by his own hand. Maybe those two tragic men and their deformed lives explain in part why I was once reluctant to marry my favorite person.

I've historically been frugal and unsentimental, accustomed to life in or near poverty. I found the prospect of a free wedding band irresistible, whatever its provenance. But the gold alloy irritated my skin. After twelve hours of wearing it, the skin at the base of my ring finger would peel as if after a sunburn. It didn't help that I dislike jewelry in general. Two or three intermittent attempts over three decades to wear a watch had ended in the waste of fifty dollars. So I didn't wear that dead man's gold band often. Mostly I wore it when I traveled, having heard the stories about casual dalliances on the road and wanting no part of them. My daughter bought me a tiny sarcophagus at an Egyptian exhibit in Idaho once, and I used that odd relic as a storage box for the ring when I was giving my finger a break.

As it happened, the sarcophagus lost its contents in a hotel somewhere in Philadelphia, nineteen years into our marriage. I suspect it fell into a crack somewhere when the sarcophagus tipped over. Whatever the cause, the ring was gone. It had joined our fathers in a realm of lost things.

I felt like a living cliché, a middle-aged man who had lost his wedding ring in a hotel. It was, no less, the wedding ring given by a man who had an affair while his wife was pregnant with their first child. I had hated the bulk of it on my hand and the rash when I wore it. But I needed to replace the band, to start a new story. Modest searching and a willingness to annoy a "sales ambassador" resulted in a 3mm titanium ring that fit my finger well. It cost less than a cheap watch, and it glistened on my hand.

The new ring is a day old. It rests nervously on my finger as she and I hold hands across the altar. The scrap of metal is cheap but clean. This tiny object tells me that I have made peace with our peers and predecessors who have used similar rings to indicate publicly to whom they were bound. I'm giddy with this ring, in this temple, at this altar. It's as if we got reengaged and remarried in the space of a day. This time I am giving her my whole heart. My soul belongs to us here, as we inhabit eternity. This is my promise; this is my faithfulness.

Hungry

'm hungry. Dying from starvation maybe, I mutter to an empty kitchen.

It's been twenty hours since I ate last. My belly tells me that a decent person wouldn't punish it this way. Food is still four hours away, according to my estimate of the time remaining for my formal fast. This state seems biologically perverse to me. Something is clearly wrong here.

But I'm fasting. So I wait.

That name, "fasting," has always struck me as inappropriate because few simple things so easily disrupt the normal flow of life as failing to eat. Especially when I'm out of practice, each hour drags me forward by the pit of my stomach. It's not the slow tempo of dread. In my heart, I know that I won't die from malnutrition and its associated plagues. But time moves at a tortuous pace on fast Sunday: I'm no good at being quiet.

Hungry and restless, my mind wonders why I'm doing this to myself all over again. This quiet is painful. I have the same problem with prayer. My soul can't sit still. It's like a two-year-old boy trying to endure sacrament meeting with the adults. The quiet frightens me. It's not natural.

When I was a young missionary, I thought fasting was a way to shout a prayer. If you wanted something too weighty to be secured by time on your knees, then you dialed the amplifier up to eleven by skipping two meals. Even the half-deaf God of the Psalms could surely hear such a shouted petition. That strategy fit well with my lifelong fear of silence, and it contributed to my general exhaustion by the end of my mission. I was hell-bent on wearing myself out in the service of the Lord.

I'm less convinced now that God needs a hearing aid. I suspect that God hears perfectly well, whether we shout or whisper. Not that we shouldn't pray with passion. Often, we must. But sometimes we will instead need to be quiet.

After my mission, I went through a phase where I thought of fasting exclusively as a method to honor the poor. I was spiritually depleted. I only had the energy to see the material, practical implications of religion. I understood the two meals without food as a way to turn a sympathetic eye to the plight of the penniless. I donated to the food bank, paid a fast offering, and tried to keep the hungry in mind. Fasting was a way to walk in a hungry person's sneakers for the proverbial mile. I still believe that, with my whole soul. There's just more to it.

The fast is not simply a story about the human toll of poverty, however important that story is. The fast is also a story about noisy excess. With the ancients, we heard Jehovah promise that the righteous would find "a land flowing with milk and honey" (Exodus 3:17). And in place of that promised land, we have built a nutritional Tower of Babel. This modern temple on the Plain of Shinar (see Genesis 11) is a cornucopia of loud, flavorless, anonymous food that swells our bellies. The ancients were so vulnerable to hunger that they sometimes saw God as mostly a story about full stomachs. We have built their longed-for Shangri-La, and it has left us achingly overweight and indigested. Our backs are breaking under the burden of our gluttony. We are never hungry, but we are always uncomfortable. We are not quiet.

But we are called to be quiet. After they established the world we know, our Heavenly Parents and their newly human children *rested*. They observed the Sabbath. They let the world fall sacredly silent.

The pattern of Sabbath as cosmic quiet has begun to shape my aspirations for the fast. When I celebrate the Sabbath, I step outside the flow of secular time. I admit to myself and to others with the methodical sequence of Sundays that the succession of earthy moments is not all there is. I tell myself, my neighbors, and God that I know there's more to the story than just atoms and quantum fields, flesh and bones, minutes and hours. I seek also those pregnant moments in which I become open to divine vastness.

In fasting, I fashion in my body the same susceptibility to God that Sunday works on my calendar. The aching beauty of mortality comes both from fleeting weakness and the eternity within which it is staged. I cannot know myself if I stay locked in the prison of flesh and bones. I step outside that prison on a Sabbath. On a fast Sunday, I strive to move outside the current of time and the crush of mortality. I am, however briefly, drawn out of the flow of energy through ecosystems and the battles of nature red in tooth and claw. I am, in a word, quiet. I become more than I seem to be.

When I fast these days, I acknowledge that I am more than an animal. I am also a human being. I hear people say, apparently sincerely, that we humans are just animals. That's an odd thing to say, like a jet pilot claiming that airplanes don't fly or an English professor pretending she is illiterate. In the very act of wondering whether we might merely be animals, we are exercising our distinction from those physical beings who have never pondered existence. I don't mean that our distinction from animals lies only in our mental capacity—there's vastly more to us than our brains and minds. But the fact of our wondering matters, and fasting calls me to such wonders.

Fasting opens up to my view the gorgeous paths that lead away from the secular highway, littered with roadkill, and into forests and mountains and hidden alpine lakes. Fasting leads me to the quiet places where sense can be made of that life we share at most partially with animals.

When I fast, I admit that I and the people I love are merely human and also more than human. We are, in a word, gods of flesh and bone. For us mortals, to be a god means to be present in both time and eternity, as physical beings who yearn and look beyond our physicalness. Being hungry means knowing that I don't wholly belong here. There's more to me than this body of myoglobin, myelin, and calcium. Uncomfortable through hunger with my all-too-mortal flesh and bones, I realize that we are all more than we seem to be. We bear the marks of eternity deep in those very bones. Like the ancient Hebrews that Jeremiah saw so clearly (see Jeremiah 31:33), we have the divine presence inscribed inside us, like a Torah scroll beating in our chest. When we fast, quietly, we find ourselves a little better able to read the word of God on that scroll.

The Place I Go to Cry

"Wait, did Dad just cry? We aren't at church. Why is he crying?" my teenage daughter teased when I got misty-eyed beside her in a movie theater. The film was probably *Coco*, the intimate story of a young musician finding his ancestors. I'm not afraid to let my eyes moisten a little when a movie moves me. But I don't normally give in to actual teardrops. I'm pretty sure I wasn't crying then, but who's to say? Some movies are powerful, and *Coco* is one of them.

My wife laughed at the comment. We both knew it was true: my kids only see me cry in one place. I'm a mostly lapsed cynic and misanthrope, and with rare exceptions (especially that first blessed year of belief in college), I haven't thought of myself as sentimental. By nature, I'm a scientist who prefers to think rigorously. I suspect that few people who know me professionally would expect me to be prone to tears.

But I cry at church. It's sort of become my thing these last few years. It's not where I expected to end up, but here I am. And it doesn't feel bad to me.

I remember talking faith with my mom's dad a few years before he died of a hemorrhage at the base of his brain. We were both scientists—he a senior biochemist and professor emeritus at the University of Minnesota with a passion for fermented dairy, and I a budding data scientist curious about life-threatening infections. We were both devout Latter-day Saints in our own odd ways. Looking back, I realize now that Granddad was a thoroughgoing modernist. His God was perhaps a bit more engaged than the God of Deism, but any divine involvement with the world had to come through science and rationality. Granddad was happiest serving as a ward clerk, where he could manage data, generate reports, and make sure the trains ran on time.

"The thing I can't abide," he told me, "is the crybabies." I want to be clear—Granddad was gentle, kind, loving, and patient. I couldn't imagine a better grandfather. He often told me that he loved me and was glad for a hug. But he didn't like what he saw as the cheap sentimentalism of tears on command. Testimony meetings drove him to distraction. In that conversation, I agreed with him. We shared what we saw as the rationalist's cool detachment. I relished the feeling that we had this special view on the world in common. We despised the maudlin tears that flowed from Latter-day Saint pulpits, especially, but not exclusively, on the first Sunday of the month.

I was a receptive audience for my grandfather's complaints. I didn't understand why people cried the way they did in church. It seemed like cheap group therapy at best, and mawkish performance art at worst. I didn't get it and didn't want to. I enjoyed the disdainful smirk I shared with Granddad.

Nowadays I'm not so sure the two of us were right back then. I hope Granddad's okay with this change in my understanding. I'd hate to imagine him cringing at his ward clerk's chair in the world of spirits when I cry at church. In my defense, there are legitimate things to cry about, real tragedies that I witness at work or engage with directly among those I love. The tragedies pile up as I grow older and love more mortals. Tears make more sense to me now than they did then. But still, there's something about Church.

As I think about Granddad's memory (he was a war veteran who loved physical exercise and would have been a formidable opponent even in his eighties, so I challenge him with some trepidation), I find the scholar in me wondering why I cry at church now and why Granddad might have despised it.

Three main themes come to my mind. For me, the tears are about vulnerability. They're about family. And they're about encounters with the divine. I'm sure there are many more reasons why people might cry at church, including depression, cultural expectations, stage fright, the provision of a channel for the expression of pent-up emotions, and the fact that church can be a place where we are encouraged to share the stories that matter most to us. The reasons for the tears are multiple and personal. Many of us will mean different things by it. And I'm aware that some will fear the shedding of tears at church. I thus speak from my own experience with church tears.

This world of ours, built on the infrastructure of market capitalism and a social Darwinist meritocracy, requires strong backs, agile minds, and skilled hands. We are told, constantly, that we are in a battle from which only the fittest will emerge. As part of this human sorting based on strength and capability, labor markets draw us from our hometowns to large cities. Increasingly we live among strangers, our families remote from us. In the midst of strangers and competitors, and ever at risk for losing our tentative purchase on success, we find our communities of trust growing smaller. Vulnerability is a virtue that seems spectacularly ill-suited to this world of ours. To show weakness is to suggest that we do not belong, that someone is coming to displace us from our precarious life.

But there's nothing about us, either our bodies or our spirits, that is designed for invulnerability. Even if it were possible to achieve, invulnerability would not bring flourishing. This is something I have had to learn repeatedly in life. If anything, our best hope for actual flourishing is recovering interdependent weakness with others and an ultimate shared dependence on God. Although it's unfortunately not true for everyone—a fact that I mourn—church offers me this kind of vulnerability in spades. I rub up next to other people who are like family, with all my struggles and ugly spots visible. This intimate village teaches me that my skin is permeable. My ward members can have an influence on me; they can witness my weakness. When we're doing religion right, we are able to open our souls to each other, often. Such vulnerability sends a spasm through my heart. For some of us, including me, that spasm can express itself in tears. I welcome the experience of vulnerability and the ways it opens my heart to other people. The wet cheeks are a reasonable price to pay for such a saving grace. I do not need to hide my emotions here, or be ashamed to express my sadness outside the sterile confines of a professional therapist's office. At church I am allowed to confess what I'm not and what I wish I were. I am allowed to admit that sometimes I ache.

Closely related to vulnerability is the promise within the Church that I can come together with others as family. Sometimes in the public rhetoric of the Church we sound as if the Victorian family nucleus is all we have energy for, but that's not what we're actually saying. The notion of family is more expansive in our past, present, and future as Saints. As a Latter-day Saint, I know that when I speak of my ward family I mean that in the gospel, people are bound to each other by more than trivial attachments. When I am with family, I can leave myself open to the full range of human emotion, including tears. I do not have to earn my status with family. That's what family means. It means that our status is born with us.

We no more need to earn our standing as Saints than we need to earn our human DNA. This sense of family that comes automatically within the ward resists the Darwinist meritocracy that otherwise wants to swallow us up. The existence of this family and its unearned and unconditional attention makes the confession of vulnerability possible for me.

These first two reasons for tears are, by and large, practical matters. They'd make sense of my willingness to shed tears even if there were no more to the Church than its capacity to build earthly communities. I do not underestimate the power of this-worldly communities. But, as with so much of life, there's more here than we are usually prone to think and see. The extra dimension matters, perhaps more than anything else. I think that sometimes—the best times—I cry because I have come into contact with an essence that lives beyond my easy capacity to understand. I'm not always clear what the right term is to designate that essence beyond, but Holy Ghost, Spirit of Christ, divine presence, or God all seem reasonable approximations. When I am actually in that divine presence, I feel my strength crumble. I'm not up to the task of sustained contact with divinity. As much as I am drawn to God's presence, I know that I cannot, as a mortal, live there permanently.

Our ancestors were more forthright about the risks of mortal proximity to the divine. As we remembered in an earlier essay, the Hebrew Bible warns that such proximity is fatal to humans; the New Testament suggests that "transfiguration" is necessary to allow such exposure. The Prophet Joseph Smith preached that something called translation was necessary to encounter the full presence of God. Each of these states is unusual, even extraordinary. In my natural state, I cannot abide God's presence. I see why the scriptures teach that mortals can't tolerate the entire presence of God. The tiny little slivers of God that I find at church reduce me to wordless tears. I sometimes imagine encountering more than that—I think my mind would burst. But this risk ought not keep me from pushing toward a little more time in the company of the divine.

A variety of responses to the vastness of divinity seem appropriate. Tears, yes, but also awe and reverence. Love, especially love. But wet eyes may be the most easily seen and reproduced. So be it. I'm okay with that. I sense that such approximation to God drives many of us to tears.

In the Church we talk a lot about feeling the Spirit, and we often do feel that Spirit in our meetings. Sometimes we act as if the Spirit exists only to stipulate which doctrines are true. Of course, the Spirit can guide us to truth. I believe that the Spirit has been integral to my faith, both its unsayable strength and its testimony to truth. But I also believe that the Spirit is about bringing us into the presence of God. When that happens to me, when I get pulled into the divine company, I find my simple verities, my poise, and my smug arrogance unsettled. This is not just the vulnerability to others that also motivates the occasional tear. This is a much deeper vulnerability to my Heavenly Parents and their divine influence. It's existential; this openness in relation goes all the way to my soul.

Vulnerability, family identity, and the divine presence. I suspect that these are the main reasons why church makes me cry. And they are among the greatest reasons I love the Church. I love that the Church provides a community in which grown men cry. I'm a little irritated now with my beloved grandfather for dismissing those tears as cheap sentimentality. As brilliant as he was as a food biochemist and as good as he was as a person, he could not have understood my tears at the pulpit. Not by a long shot. We could all stand to let ourselves abide a little more often in the company of God, even if for some of us that means that our chins will tremble and our cheeks will get wet.

Sacraments in the Time of Pestilence

Our Kwanzan cherry tree started to shed its exuberant blossoms in May. It can only hold those purple-pink flowers aloft for a few days. A splash of love and color, and then they are gone. I'm standing on the park strip in front of my family's house, in a black-and-white mask my middle daughter bought from her favorite leotard company early in the COVID-19 pandemic.

I've grown accustomed to masks by now. At first they gave me a tightness in my chest that reminded me that I sometimes imagine I've got mild asthma (the alternative is that I'm anxious, so asthma it is). But now the masks reassure me that when I am at work I will not spread a virus to the people around me. The sight of a mask on the face of another tells me that they are protecting me. These thin sheets across my mouth and nose have become a comforting misery seven weeks into the US pandemic.

I stand on the park strip now because I'm working clinically at the hospital, looking after patients. I'm not working in the COVID ICU, but the risk is higher than we will tolerate for my wife's safety. So I've temporarily quarantined myself in my friends' basement across town. I come home from work, shower, change clothes, and then drive over to the house where my family lives. I'm too busy and tired to be lonely right now, but I can tell that something deep inside me aches anyway, groans with the sadness of worlds turned upside down and bodies newly abandoned to the grave, aches with the fact that I have not touched my wife in two months.

Today is Sunday; evening has come. I am weary, but I am home for twenty awkward minutes as I shift from foot to foot on the grass beside my wife's deep-blue Jeep. My mind nervously collates the tasks that remain before I can sleep. I can't focus on much else.

My family has been waiting patiently for me to visit so that they can partake of the sacrament, our Latter-day Saint experience of the Eucharist that Jesus drew out of the Passover meal. We are devout folk. These devotions and the world they open up to our view are the dominant rhythms of our life together. We had a month or so to practice home church during the weeks when my exposure to the hospital was limited enough that I could live out my quarantine in the basement of our own home. Those early home sacraments weren't smooth. I kept saying "wine" instead of "water" during the second prayer, and I'd have to pull the text of the prayers up on my phone or computer to remember them. In this desperate time of waging scientific battle with contagion, I spend too much time with those electronic devices already. I am prone to fall back into reviewing emails or reading research studies when I should be opening my heart to God.

Watching my struggles, my youngest daughter wrote the prayers by hand on small note cards with a filigreed edge. "Wine" now reads "water," and no screen is required. Today my daughter has deposited these cards on the sidewalk and backed away. My mask on, I grab the sacrament prayers and retreat back to the idle Jeep, covered in pollen and blossom fragments. It's the same way they serve me dinner each night.

As I stand twenty feet from the four of them, bereft and yet awash in grace, I realize that it is 2020. Thirty years ago, I read the prayer on the wine-turned-to-water in a chapel in Kaysville, Utah. That prayer jolted me from one life to another. Eighteen years old, I wept my way through the prayer over the blood of Christ, filled with the love of God. Words and tears took turns for several minutes as I worked through the prayer. My adolescent atheism had come to an end.

For three decades, I have been a God-believer, an aspiring child of covenant. I date this belief to that sacred experience with the emblems of Christ's divine body made human and then made dead. That first great sacramental prayer I pronounced with my brother and friends by my side and a congregation of women and men who had helped raise me. There was personal transformation and community love in that encounter with the sacrament in 1990. That sacred history has brought me to this present day of pandemic and my resistance to it. It has brought me to this current life full of grace.

Now I am trying to speak the words of the sacramental prayer between the movements of the neighbors, none inclined to wear a face covering, happily chatting along the sidewalks. I do not want to embarrass us or them as we enact this private devotion in full view because I do not now belong inside my house.

The bunched-up fabric catches uncomfortably in my teeth as I speak sacred words through my mask. I do not experience that love and peace we call the Spirit. I feel instead that I am tired. That there is more work to do, hours more, and I am already spent. I read those beloved prayers, so simple and potent. I feel love for my family, but little else. I don't partake of the emblems that they set out on the sidewalk between us because I don't want them too close to me. The whole point of this distance is to protect them. I will not place these beloveds in harm's way.

I am too tired even to see the bathos of my self-pity on this sidewalk today. I am healthy, I am employed, I am doing the science that I love, and my family is alive and well. I am allowed to speak the prayers aloud and thereby bind this meal and this family into the many millions of times these prayers have been spoken over these emblems honoring that first Easter and the bitter days leading up to it. Even in the throes of this pandemic, I am blessed beyond measure. Many in the body of Christ are suffering far more than I am. Too many are falling into the grave. Others are forever scarred by the illness that stretched them physically between life and death. Others are alone and afraid, locked in their homes for safety. This terrible virus preys on much that is bad in humanity and all that is good. Protecting the vulnerable in our midst has meant that we keep ourselves physically apart, that we separate ourselves from hugs, close laughter, songs together, happy crowds, and concerts. It has also called us to think, strenuously, about the nature of our society and economy.

I want this sacrament to be simple and powerful, like the one thirty years ago. I want to touch my family again. God should come when and where we ask. God should be like a snuggling puppy or a warm sweater.

But I know that life and God and the world and eternity are more than our desire to choreograph them. They are wildly and beautifully and graciously beyond our easy manipulation. But they are not beyond our communion. We are yoked in covenant.

I will continue to think through this experience for weeks: the cherry blossoms, the lilt of my wife's salt-and-pepper curls, the urgent intelligence of my daughter's script, the strange ballerina's mask, the sourdough loaf made from our family starter, the ache in my neck from constant straining at computers. I will turn these images and their history over in my mind. I'm doing it now. I will think those moments from that Sunday into something beautiful, however empty I felt at that moment. And I will carry the sad poignancy of the Spirit that did not fill my heart this time as I read those ancient prayers. I will carry in my heart the sadness of my friends and neighbors at this terrible time, where I will mix their grief with the love of a God remembered in a meal of broken bread. I will bask in the sanctity and beauty of this world being remade in spring. Grief and grace will commingle in my covenanted heart, scintillating between earth and heaven.

I got tested for coronavirus a few days later—an explosion of stinging pain at the point where my nasal passages curve around my brain, forty cycles or so of an RNA amplification machine, and the reassuring word "undetected." I returned to full fellowship in my home. The cherry blossoms had melted into our ragged grass. Before I left, I had weeded out hundreds of dandelions, a reminder of my inattention last summer as they quietly and persistently spread across our yard. In retrospect, that battle with the crushing power of Darwinian evolution was a premonition of the viral catastrophe of 2020. When I returned home from my COVID-19 exile, a few insolent yellow flowers had already returned, taunting me.

But the people I love most in the world ran to me, holding me tight. I experienced the exquisite pleasure of touching a person without gloves on. I hugged again and kissed my children on the forehead, my wife on the lips. We held each other for long minutes, celebrating the physical proximity that is our defiance of the coronavirus and the world it is transforming. In a blessed week, I remembered life again.

That Sunday we celebrated the sacrament in the Uinta Mountains, the location of my first inklings of the possibility of God. Those mountains trained me to listen so that I could hear God over the sacrament in 1990. As my family and I assembled to bless the emblems of Christ's sacred meal, the Provo River shuttled the melting alpine snow past us on its way to Utah Lake. That water does not know that it will then flow along our River Jordan to our Dead Sea, the Great Salt Lake. Up here the dandelions are with their sister wildflowers in the old riverbed where we have gathered and the meadow just above it, where old horses graze and sun themselves. There it is again, that sacred vastness. Here we are, in the midst of eternity.

The night before I returned to clinical service and another temporary exile in my friends' basement, I took my youngest daughter out for a bike ride around the neighborhood. We've been trying to spend more time celebrating the informal sacraments of parenthood. She's competitive and inquisitive, and she loves horses. I think she sees bicycles as a way that we can share a simpler version of the horses she wishes she could be riding instead.

She tells me as we pedal along that she wants to ride the way I do, spine straight and hands hanging comfortably beside me. She wants to ride hands-free. As we move through the neighborhood, the sycamores bowing leaves over their greenish bark, like a haphazard quilt, she lifts one arm and then the other. The bicycle wobbles and twists. I catch up and tell her that on my mission my companions and I would kick each other's tires in jest, like an idiots' jousting competition. She takes a couple stabs at the joust. Her legs are too short, she tells me, but still manages once or twice to nearly crash our bikes.

I pull up beside her again and model for her the bend of the back, the quick movement of the shoulders that releases the hands from the bicycle. Go fast, I tell her. The forward momentum will hold you up. Keep pedaling. You'll be able to hold your hands up for longer. Keep trying a little bit at a time. That's how you'll get the hang of it.

She makes quick movements, and her bicycle jiggles for the half second her hands are aloft. We make our way past the neighborhood grocery market where—in a pre-pandemic age—we would buy a kids' serving of gelato and she would offer me a taste, to prove that we belong to each other. We bounce across the cratered asphalt of the streets, slide past the redbrick church we attended when we first arrived in Utah. Her handlebars tremble less each time she holds her hands up. I say the encouraging things I would have wanted from a father. We curve away from the wide, deep hollow through which the remnant of a mountain stream runs.

We arrive at the spot on a wide boulevard where her homeroom teacher lives. She tenses her back and pushes against the handlebars. Her hands come up, the bicycle drives true, and she pedals on. She lifts her arms in a heavenward salute. I feel the waves of smiles pouring from her body as I cycle toward her. She worships as she sings her way up the road. I do too. I praise God that we have ever lived, that there has ever been a child whose father taught her to ride hands-free. This glory rises to eternity and back.

Conclusion

This book's title is inspired by Enos in the Book of Mormon. The young prophet, whom I remember as a muscular athlete more prone to sins of the flesh than a bookish prophet like Nephi, experienced a moral crisis early in adulthood. Enos tells us that his book is the story of "the wrestle which I had before God" en route to "a remission of my sins" (Enos 1:2). There's a tendency, and Enos is prone to it, to use memoir as a way to tie a bow around a complicated life history. We want our personal histories to be perfectly even, the sides of the wrapping paper precisely symmetrical, each line of the crisp red bow centered. Enos seems to be using his scriptural memoir to make us think that there was a single "before" and a single "after": he was coarse and ungodly, he wrestled like Jacob did at Peniel, and then he was redeemed. It's a tidy package.

But then Enos lets something slip that points to a fuller account of his life. He explains that he remembered what his father had said about "eternal life, and the joy of the saints" (verse 3). These stories about life in God "sunk deep" into his heart (verse 3). These luminous truths triggered a response:

the young man's "soul hungered" (v. 4). It's natural enough to think of food as making us hungry, but I see Enos's choice of words as telling us a great deal about the experience of approaching God. For many of us, God feels inaccessible, like a force that we can strain toward but never touch. God is truly there, but God isn't fully attainable. The divine presence hovers just out of sight. We heaven-and-earth people will never be entirely where God is. Enos's hunger speaks to that experience of living in-between.

The hunter-prophet himself frames that hunger in terms of obligation to his people and his growing love for them. He continues with "many long strugglings" in his newfound religious commitment (verse 11). He "labored with all diligence" to respond to the call that love for his people demanded of him (verse 11). When Enos came to know God's grace, it was no simple transition from an evil past to a noble present. Instead of rest, he found ongoing hunger and toil. The wrestle wasn't over. Just because he knew that he had entered a covenant relationship with God didn't mean that he would stop struggling. His soul would continue to hunger.

I get Enos. It seems to me sometimes that I am always hungry and never full. But even as I say that, I know it's not entirely true. There are moments of fullness, however uncommon they may be. Sometimes, when the wind snakes its way through the leaves of the mulberry tree and the robins ask cheerfully what the night will bring, I know that I belong to God and God to me. Sometimes, when I hear my wife's voice or see the form of my daughter walking toward me with her ballet steps, I know that love permeates the universe. Occasionally, when I work my way through a knotty scripture or share true clarity in a Sunday School class, I feel a warming spirit and belief deep inside me. Most of the time, though, I live on earth and in earth. That too is a kind of sacred clarity. I know what I'm like by nature, and I know what I am in the love and light of Christ. It will take many long strugglings for me, as for Enos, to abide in God's presence. It's the work of a lifetime.

I'm also realizing that the story of my strugglings hasn't always been entirely true. It wasn't just the story of Leroy and the chemistry midterm that I got wrong. It's also the question of who I am. I've told a story about myself for most of my life. It began with a sense of isolation in a painful childhood. That story says that I am petty and cruel, that I don't feel, that I don't have any spiritual gifts to speak of. I have created this history, I think, because it's at least partly true, but some of it also is because my mind is natively designed to see the flaws in things. I'm like a bee for pollen or a bear for honey when it comes to flaws. I've been honing that skill for decades now as a physician and scientist. I don't think I'm malicious; I'm just incredibly critical. I've worked hard to calm the negativity and to use these inborn mental processes to shed more rather than less of the love of God in the world. It's a long slog through deep mud. It's been better with Jesus, but I'm still profoundly imperfect. I suspect that many of us are conflicted in similar ways. The Russian novelist and public figure Aleksandr Solzhenitsyn famously said that the line between good and evil passes through every one of us. That much feels perfectly clear to me. I have lived it from the inside. When I haven't worked hard in the company of good-hearted people and by the grace of God, I have watched myself lapse back into that natural state multiple times.

But through work—by God, by me, and by the people I love—I am no longer the man I once was. The natural Sam, that enemy to God, no longer controls me. He is part of my past, but he is not, by God, the man of my future. And here's the liberty that I haven't quite let myself acknowledge until now. I'm no longer that man, however much he haunts me day by day and however much he wants to be set free. I really am a kind and tenderhearted person. I really do love children and other people. I see that now.

As I was working on King Benjamin's sermon for a Sunday School lesson at the same time that I was writing this conclusion, I hit hard against Mosiah 2:25. Benjamin has been reminding his people that class divisions are not of God, that all people have similar dignity. Then the dying king asks, harshly, "Can ye say aught of yourselves? I answer you, Nay. Ye cannot say that ye are even as much as the dust of the earth." As a missionary, I read that passage the same way I read everything else—as evidence that I really was a tortured misanthrope, no better than dirt. But reading it again with an eye to the world's sabbath and the transformation that lives in Christ, I saw that dirt is lovely and life-giving. I remembered that on the threshold of that glorious seventh day, God declared dirt and dust and soil and all that lives among them "good" (Genesis 1:25). And flawed human beings, like me and like those who heard King Benjamin's sermon, he declared to be "*very* good" (Genesis 1:31). God's statement on the verge of the world's first Sabbath is a passionate note that rumbles across all time and space and finds its eternal place in Christ's life and death and life again. As with Enos, the struggle and the glory comes as I turn my mind to others. I am good, and that goodness takes a lot of work. There is work to do because there's a difference between being good like a waterfall or a stand of aspens is good, and being good the way a human being can be good.

This hovering between good and evil and the natural and the artificial mirrors another hovering. It's the one that I've adopted as the theme for this book. We hover between heaven and earth. Sometimes I think we get tempted by extremes: we want to live wholly in the earth—attending to prosperity and pleasure and the simple things like Costco runs and family hikes and a solid paycheck and comfortable-maybe-even-fashionable clothing. In an extreme version, this is what people describe as the modern secular worldview: There is nothing but this earth that matters. That's one extreme, an attempt to live an earth-only life. The other is to live only in heaven, to imagine that nothing in this world matters, that when Jesus returns all will be made right, so it doesn't matter what happens along the way. Let the world burn; it had it coming. That's the other extreme, the proclamation of a heaven-only life.

But I am called to live between heaven and earth, and I am grateful for the call. There was a proverb we repeated for a while when I was younger. Our goal as Saints was to be "in the world but not of the world" (see John 17:14). I see where the phrase meant to point. We had to be present here in the world. We had to go to work, drive cars, and participate in broader society. But our hearts would be somewhere else. I don't think that saying is wrong, although I am not sure it goes far enough. We need to be of the world, but we need to also be of heaven. That's what I mean by the hovering, flickering, or scintillating. It's this sense that we are really both, but not simply or always simultaneously. It's tense sometimes, this having two passports, this belonging to two worlds, but that's what God wants. And that's what Restoration theology is all about. Even God is a citizen of both realms, and so are we. Heaven and earth come together in me and in the divine love within which I have my being. Sometimes it takes all the power I have in my wobbly legs to hold it all together. I'm not always successful at it. But that is what I'm made for; that is where my soul hungers.

Index

About the Author

Samuel Morris Brown is associate professor of pulmonary and critical care medicine and medical ethics and humanities at the University of Utah and an intensive care physician in the Shock Trauma ICU at Intermountain Medical Center. His award-winning book *In Heaven as It Is on Earth: Joseph Smith and the Early Mormon Conquest of Death* was published by Oxford University Press in 2012. He is also the author of *First Principles and Ordinances: The Fourth Article of Faith in Light of the Temple*, a 2014 Neal A. Maxwell Institute Living Faith publication. Sam and his wife, Kate Holbrook, are raising three daughters in Salt Lake City.